"Every single recipe has a human story to it,
and that story has to be told."

—Charles Masson, Restaurateur

THE *GOD'S LOVE WE DELIVER COOKBOOK*
IS MADE POSSIBLE THROUGH THE GENEROUS SUPPORT OF

The Palette Fund and Terrence Meck
in honor of Rand Skolnik

CORPORATE AND FOUNDATION SUPPORT

Bloomingdale's
Steven & Alexandra Cohen Foundation
The Aaron and Betty Gilman Family Foundation
Bob & Eileen Gilman Family Foundation
Klingenstein Fields Wealth Advisors
Michael Kors
Dorothea Leonhardt Fund of Communities Foundation of Texas
Ralph Lauren
William M. & Miriam F. Meehan Foundation
May and Samuel Rudin Family Foundation

INDIVIDUAL SUPPORT

Marisa Arango
Michael Kors and Lance LePere
Karen Pearl
Michael A. Sennott
Lesley and Brian Sondey
David A. Terveen
Blaine Trump and Steven Simon

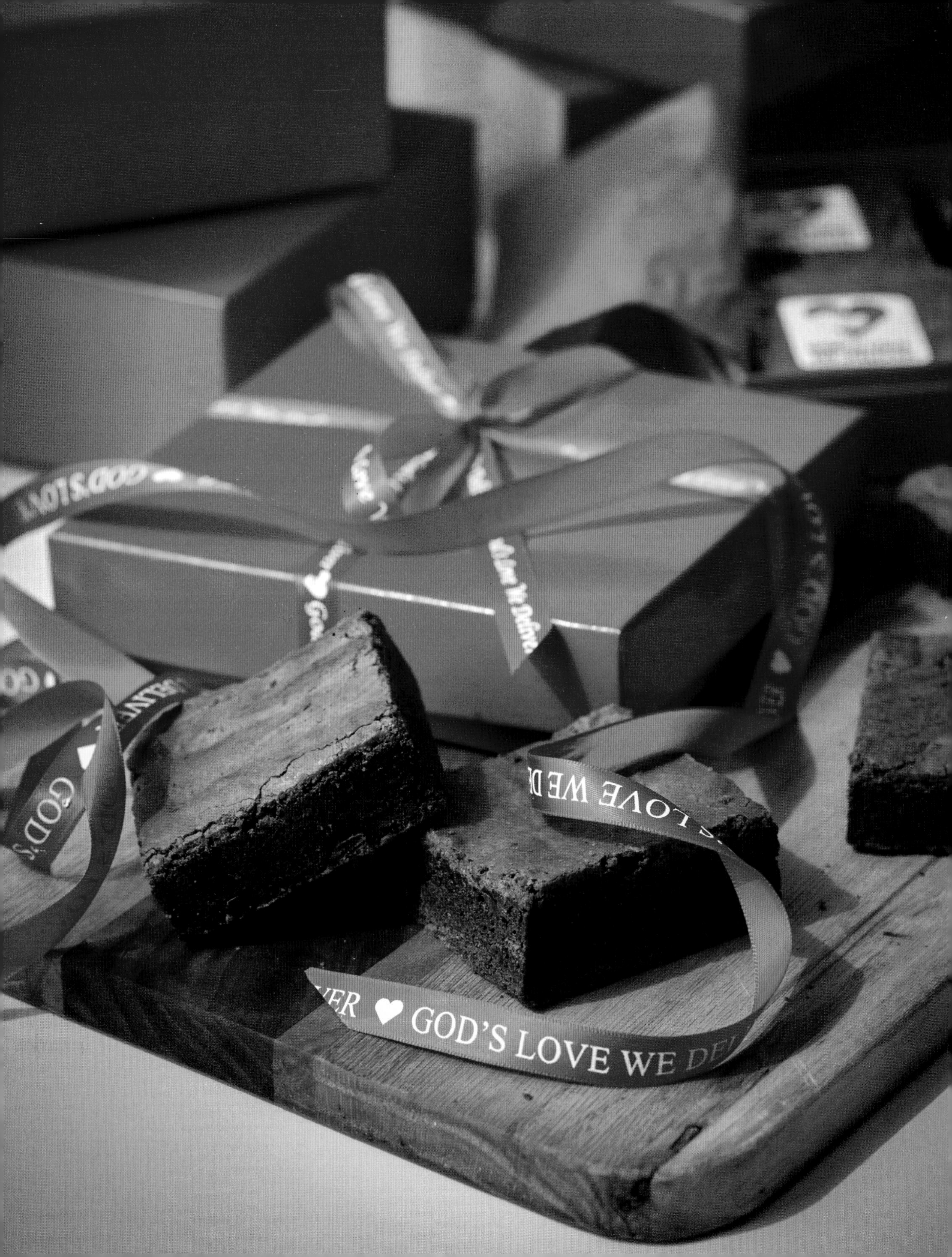
VER ♥ GOD'S LOVE WE DE
LOVE WE DE

GOD'S LOVE WE DELIVER COOKBOOK

Nourishing Stories and Recipes from Notable Friends

Compiled by Jon Gilman and Christopher Idone
Introduction by Ina Garten

FOOD PHOTOGRAPHY BY BEN FINK

A WELCOME ENTERPRISES BOOK

GOD'S LOVE WE DELIVER

NEW YORK

PREFACE

Sometimes, as every cook knows, even an oven mishap can end in something good. I experienced one such accident three years ago and it's one of the reasons you're holding this book in your hands today.

In late August 2012, at my home in Sag Harbor, NY, a blackberry cobbler I was preparing with my good friend and noted cookbook author Christopher Idone bubbled over, sizzling and smoking on the hot oven floor. As I scurried to clean up the sticky mess, the aroma instantly transported me back to my childhood in Seattle.

In the summer, once the gray shroud from the Puget Sound cleared away, the city was bathed in hot, shimmering sun for three blissful months. With the heat came a flush of fruit-filled blackberry bushes. With thorns as big as talons, these brutes pushed through sidewalks, strangled fences, and turned vacant lots into jungles of tangled vines so thick that "dogs and small children are sometimes engulfed and never heard from again," as fellow Washingtonian Tom Robbins put it.

By August, when the temperature hit 90 degrees, my two sisters, my brother, and I, cranky with the impending start of school, would start bickering about nothing at all. That was when my exasperated mother would toss four buckets at us and march us up the hill to collect the plump berries. Back at home, Mom would first dress our wounds, and then she'd set to whipping our haul into the world's sweetest, tartest, juiciest cobbler.

When the whiff of burning blackberry juice flooded my senses that afternoon in 2012, those distant memories rushed back into my consciousness. When I mentioned this to Christopher, his eyes lit up. "It's true," he said. "Cooking today is so often seen as some abstract overwrought enterprise. But one of the most overlooked aspects of eating and sharing food is the way it triggers sense memory." And that was how this book was born.

I am a board member of God's Love We Deliver and that conversation made it clear that creating a cookbook celebrating stories and recipes that connect to past experiences and emotions would be a great testament to what this organization stands for.

By the end of the evening, Christopher and I had drawn up a wish list of contributors: chefs, artists, writers, actors, musicians, public figures, and other notable friends of God's Love. Over the next two years we collected recipes for the dishes that evoked their most tender, funny, sad, or inspiring recollections. We also learned some surprising and delightful things about them:

Serene Green farm stand in Sag Harbor, NY.

Isabella Rossellini's mom, Ingrid Bergman, a brilliant actress but decidedly less brilliant cook, made cookies so hard her kids couldn't bite through them; Rosanne Cash is so deeply passionate about her coconut cake that she wants it served at her funeral; and the great French restaurateur Charles Masson once romanced his wife with the "perfect" scrambled egg—just to mention a few.

Today, I'm pleased to offer you this collection of recipes (all of which have been tested, so yes, they work) and the stories that conjure that other powerful emotion so often associated with food: love. And thanks to the generous support of so many individuals, corporations, and foundations, the production costs of this beautiful cookbook have been covered in full. That means that 100 percent of the proceeds go directly to feeding the thousands of God's Love clients who are too sick to shop or cook for themselves.

Sadly, Christopher died before the book was published. He fought a long battle with cancer, but up until the end, food remained one of his great pleasures. Every Sunday evening my husband and I would bring him a home-cooked supper. To this day when I drive up the street to the farmer who sells his eggs in a cooler by the side of the road in Sag Harbor, I often think of Christopher and the enormous joy that cooking simple fresh ingredients—even a soft-boiled egg—always brought to him.

This book is dedicated to his memory.

JON GILMAN

CONTENTS

117 PASTA & GRAINS

151 SEAFOOD

181 POULTRY & MEAT

235 DESSERTS

INTRODUCTION

Thirty years ago, a hospice volunteer named Ganga Stone visited an AIDS patient named Richard. Little did she know, that experience would change not only her life, but also the lives of millions of New Yorkers. Wanting to be of some help, Ganga delivered a bag of groceries to Richard's apartment. Returning the next day to find the groceries still on the counter, Ganga realized that he was too ill to cook for himself, so she decided to bring him a homemade meal on her next visit. Ganga understood that something as simple as offering a freshly prepared meal to a person in need would not only bring them critical nutrition but also the compassion of someone who cares about them. One day, while delivering a meal, she was stopped by a minister in the neighborhood who asked her what she was doing. After she told him, he said, "You're not just delivering food, you're delivering God's love." And so, God's Love We Deliver was born.

Three decades later, with an expanded mission to include people living with any life-altering illness, God's Love cooks and delivers 1.5 million meals a year to more than 6,000 individuals. Every meal is specifically designed and planned for each client by a registered nutrition dietitian, because God's Love realizes that every person with a severe illness has a different nutritional requirement. For those GLWD serves, food is much more than just sustenance—it's also medicine. Good nutrition helps people heal faster. So basic but so important.

That information alone demonstrates the incredible difference that God's Love makes in the New York City community, but the fact that 10,000 volunteers show up every year to cook, bake, pack, and deliver all those meals is equally astounding. Consider this: someone personally delivers every single meal with a warm smile to each client—on nearly every day of the year. I have chopped vegetables in the God's Love kitchen in SoHo alongside some of these dedicated men and women, and I can tell you it is an inspiring and heartwarming experience.

Because God's Love knows that illness affects the whole family, they also provide meals for the caregivers and children of their clients-—complete with a menu of kid-friendly dishes. They even send a personalized cake to each client on his or her birthday! One man wrote to tell them that his wife had died and he was home alone and ill. He had completely forgotten that it was his birthday until a beautiful young woman showed up with a cake inscribed with his name, and he was overwhelmed with gratitude. How lovely is that?

Jon Gilman, Ina Garten, and David Ludwigson volunteering in the God's Love kitchen, September, 2015.

Though not precisely a cake, this beautiful cookbook is a delicious celebration of God's Love's 30th birthday, complete with their name on top. It is a tribute to the simple but powerful notion that is at the core of the organization's guiding philosophy: Food is love. As someone who makes her living feeding others, I know very intimately how true this is. Every recipe has been contributed by a prominent supporter of God's Love (including me!) and is accompanied by a personal memory, story, or musing that reflects how meaningful, comforting, or even life-changing a home-cooked meal can be.

I hope you'll enjoy cooking from this collection of marvelous recipes and reading these stories from the heart—and I also hope you'll consider giving to God's Love We Deliver, so that people who are ill can continue to receive nutritional meals along with the extraordinary compassion of this remarkable organization. I couldn't be prouder of my involvement with God's Love, or more certain of their profound and positive impact.

INA GARTEN, Barefoot Contessa cookbooks and television

BREAKFAST

APRIL BLOOMFIELD
Chef

I love this porridge recipe because it always reminds me of my granddad. He used to make the best porridge (aka oatmeal, in the States). His porridge was never too runny or too thick—it was always just right. My granddad had that way about him, always preparing things just right.

The rolled oats simmering in milk smell so sweet and inviting that, to this day, I go all fuzzy inside just thinking about it. This is still one of my most beloved dishes for a cold morning when the ground is frosty—it is always comforting and almost makes you not want to leave the house. My favorite part, still, is pouring milk into the spaces around the edges of the bowl—the cool milk hitting the hot porridge, making it set like a custard. This part of the process especially reminds me of my dear granddad, it is like getting a great big hug from him every time I have it. I can guarantee it will warm you from the inside out on even the chilliest and dreariest of days.

Porridge

Serves 2

1 ½ cups whole milk, more for serving or reheating

1 ½ cups water

1 ½ teaspoons flaky sea salt, such as Maldon, or ¾ teaspoon kosher salt

½ cup steel-cut oats

½ cup old-fashioned rolled oats

2 tablespoons maple sugar, brown sugar, granulated sugar, or maple syrup, according to preference

Leftover porridge is good reheated with a little extra milk or water.

1. Combine the milk, water, and salt in a 2- to 3-quart pot and bring to a boil over high heat. Add both kinds of oats and lower the heat to maintain a simmer. Cook, stirring frequently, until the rolled oats are mushy and the steel-cut oats are just tender, about 20 minutes.

2. Taste the oatmeal; it should be salty. Add sugar or syrup to taste. Pour into bowls and let stand for a minute. Pour a little cold milk around the edge of each bowl so it pools. Add a five-finger pinch of sugar or drizzle of syrup in the center of each and let it melt; serve right away.

LAUREN GRAHAM

Actor, writer

"I always judge a restaurant by the quality of its bread," my father, a strict toast-in-the-morning man, is fond of saying. According to him, the bread should be warm and crusty, welcoming, and a little decadent. Growing up, I was taught the breadbasket was an exciting indication of the meal to come, a *happy* thing.

But I live in Los Angeles now, where bread is something to be tolerated but feared, like traffic jams, or wrinkles. Unlike New York, we didn't invent the bagel or the cronut, items everyone can agree are justifiable deviations from the gluten-free paleo juice cleanse we're all supposedly on. We do have a lot of cupcake shops in LA, which might make us seem "fun" to out-of-towners, but everyone knows those are used only when you're sucking up to your agent, or

as hostess gifts at parties, where no one except the kids will eat them. I always feel bad in Los Angeles when I see the waiter heading to our table with the basket of bread, which I already know will be rejected by my dining companions, brushed away with a wave that, while polite, also implies he's *got* to be joking. When every precious calorie is being counted and logged into an iPhone app, how can anyone allow themselves the luxury, the downright recklessness, of spending those precious points on something as unnecessary as a *roll*?

But I've found one exception, one bread iteration that *no one* ever says no to, that everyone in fact requests with the jittery tone of the wildly carb-deprived: "You're making those bread thingies at Thanksgiving again this year,

right? RIGHT?" It's true that we can't seem to agree on whether these "bread thingies" are Yorkshire puddings or popovers—it all depends on whether you use drippings or butter, and the size of the pan. But in any case, they make a spectacular impression, even though they're surprisingly quick and easy to prepare.

I had my first popover at a small inn in Maine where my father and I would stay sometimes when I was in elementary school, on yearly ski trips with my cousin and uncle. The inn was small, I realize now, but through my 10-year-old eyes it seemed huge, a castle to get lost in, find secret hiding places, and roam gleefully un-parented. The innkeepers allowed us into the kitchen sometimes, where we'd help ourselves to glass after glass of milk from a giant stainless-steel dispenser. And at dinner, the breadbasket was full of piping-hot popovers. I didn't know from calories then, and probably had two or three at a sitting. Youth!

You can buy a pan specifically made for them, but as much as I love purchasing nonessential kitchen items from Sur La Table, they're just fine in a regular muffin tin. Even when they don't rise perfectly, they taste amazing and are delicious with gravy at a holiday meal or with butter and jam for breakfast. Even the most gluten-phobic among you will have to agree they are, like the breadbaskets of my childhood, a happy thing.

Popovers

Makes 12

1½ tablespoons unsalted butter, melted, plus softened butter for greasing pans

1½ cups all-purpose flour, sifted

¾ teaspoon kosher salt

3 extra-large eggs, at room temperature

1½ cups whole milk, at room temperature

There are three secrets to great popovers: 1) Make sure the pan is hot before you pour in the batter; 2) fill each section no more than half way (here it's actually less than half full); and 3) no peeking. They're much easier than you'd expect, and they make any meal feel festive.

1. Preheat the oven to 425°F.

2. Generously grease a 12-cup popover pan or large muffin tin with softened butter. Place the pan in the oven for 2 minutes to preheat.

3. Meanwhile, whisk together the melted butter, flour, salt, eggs, and milk until smooth. The batter will be thin.

4. Fill the popover cups less than half way with batter and bake until golden brown, 25 to 30 minutes. No peeking until 25 minutes. Continue to bake if still light in color. Remove from oven and serve hot.

KYLE MacLACHLAN
Actor

When I was a youngster, my brothers and I always looked forward to my dad's special weekend breakfasts. He would get up extra early, preparing fruit, fresh orange juice, bacon, and Bisquick batter to make pancakes or waffles for his three sons. It was a feast.

It's only as I've gotten older and become a father myself that I realize how much my dad expressed his love for us through this simple ritual of a homemade morning meal. Like father, like son: I now do the same for my boy. I feel closer to my dad as I cook my son Callum's breakfast. I also understand that my son won't truly appreciate what's behind my effort until he too becomes a father, juicing the oranges and whipping up a batch of waffle batter for his children. And so it goes…

Yeasted Waffles

Makes about 4 large (6-inch) waffles

¼ cup warm water

1½ teaspoons active-dry yeast

1 tablespoon plus a pinch of granulated sugar

¼ cup unsalted butter, melted

1 cup whole or 2 percent milk (if you've got it, buttermilk is also a great option)

½ teaspoon salt

½ teaspoon vanilla extract

1½ cups all-purpose flour

¼ teaspoon baking soda

1 large egg

Cooking spray for the waffle iron

1. Prepare batter the night before. Put the water in a large mixing bowl (the batter will double in size as it rises), and stir in the yeast and pinch of sugar. Let stand for a few minutes, until foamy (if it doesn't foam, start again with new yeast).

2. Melt the butter over low heat or in the microwave. Combine the butter with the milk, salt, vanilla, and remaining tablespoon of sugar. Test with your finger to make sure the mixture has cooled to lukewarm, and then stir it into the dissolved yeast mixture. Add the flour and stir until it forms a thick, shaggy dough and no more flour is visible.

3. Cover the bowl with plastic wrap and put it in the fridge. The batter will double in volume as it rises.

4. The next morning, remove the batter from the fridge about an hour before you plan to use it.

5. Preheat the oven to 200°F.

6. Stir the baking soda into the batter. Separate the egg, putting the white in a bowl and the yolk into the batter. Beat the egg white with a whisk just to firm peaks and fold into the batter along with the yolk.

7. Make the waffles according to the waffle-iron manufacturer's instructions, greasing both sides of the iron with cooking spray. As they cook, transfer them to a large rimmed baking sheet and keep warm in the oven in one layer until ready to serve.

8. Serve with butter, maple syrup, crisp bacon, and fresh-squeezed orange juice.

MARIO BATALI

Chef, restaurateur, television host, cookbook author

My kids gifted me a cookbook of their very own back on my fiftieth birthday and it's the best present I have ever received. Benno, Leo, and their mother, Susi, who acted as professional photographer, spent all summer crafting new recipes they thought I would enjoy. They've always been in the kitchen cooking alongside me, just as I was in the kitchen with my grandmother when I was incredibly young. So it's no shock to me that they have taken cooking up on their own, and that their recipes are delicious and simple and make me misty-eyed as a proud father.

Brown Sugar Pancakes

Serves 6 (makes 12 to 14 pancakes)

2 cups all-purpose flour

1 tablespoon baking powder

1 pinch kosher salt

1 tablespoon granulated sugar

2 tablespoons unsalted butter, plus more for the pan and for serving

2 eggs

2 cups whole milk

½ teaspoon vanilla extract

3 tablespoons light brown sugar

Maple syrup

1. Put a nonstick or cast-iron frying pan on the stove over medium heat.

2. In a medium bowl, mix the flour, baking powder, salt, and granulated sugar together.

3. Melt 2 tablespoons of the butter and set aside. In a large bowl, beat the eggs with the milk. Add the vanilla and the melted butter, then whisk some more.

4. Whisk the dry ingredients into the wet ingredients in thirds, making sure to get all the lumps out of the batter. Crumble 2 tablespoons of the brown sugar on top of the batter and whisk in.

5. Melt some butter in the pan until it bubbles. Cook the pancakes in batches: Pour the batter onto the pan (not all of it, just a ladleful at a time—we like a 2- or 3-ounce ladle) so you form good round circles. Flip the pancakes when bubbles form on the top, and cook them till they are golden underneath and just cooked through.

6. Sprinkle the remaining tablespoon of brown sugar over the pancakes and serve hot, with maple syrup and butter.

CHARLES MASSON

Restaurateur

I believe true luxury begins with comfort, and real comfort is born out of simplicity. Simplicity is not an easy thing to achieve. It is much easier to juggle a lot of ingredients, do a lot of razzmatazz, and impress guests with decoration and fluff. Someone who is so sincere as to cook the perfect egg or roast the perfect chicken will not garner headlines. Yet, it is something that all of us love to have and return to time and again. You never get tired of a soufflé. You never get tired of a broth when it's done perfectly. Or pomme purée. There are some dishes that are classics because their composition by definition is modern.

My father could whip up anything with just what was in the refrigerator. He could take an old carrot, half an onion, a lemon, a leftover piece of chicken and a few bones and make the best soup in the world. He was a man who understood what having little meant. I think that kind of a discipline is phenomenal.

Look at the great masters and painters—like Goya, El Greco, Rembrandt, Velazquez. Examine their palettes and read their diaries. What you will find is revealing: they did not use very many paints. I'm sure they could have mixed as many colors as they liked, but in essence their palettes consisted of mainly three or four paint tubes. With just that, they were able to compose great harmonies on the canvas. I believe the relationship between making art, planting a garden, and cooking are intricately woven together. If you observe nature enough, you're going to want to paint with it, to take a few vegetables and herbs that are in season and make a feast out of them.

But today there are just too many distractions. Many of the young chefs I meet now can get anything they want from any part of the planet. What this does is it totally erases their connection with nature. It makes them forget the seasons; there are too many ingredients, and it becomes a cacophony. You lose the identity of the cuisine and the ancestry of the dish, and you end up with what's called "fusion cuisine." To me, fusion cuisine equals confusion cuisine. Make up

your mind. Every single recipe has a human story to it, and that story has to be told.

The first thing my father taught me in the kitchen was how to scramble an egg. I know it sounds ridiculous, but a scrambled egg can be fantastic or disastrous. Because there are so few ingredients, and so few emergency exits if it goes wrong. It must be on the verge of being uncooked, yet it has to have form and shape. The key is the fire. To know when to turn it off. It has a lot more to do with technique than anything else. Once you hit the perfect temperature, it's chemistry. It is a transformation of the most basic ingredients into something absolutely delicious. It's not complicated—in fact, it's stupidly simple, and that's what I love about it—but I've seen a lot of cooks make a hash out of it.

I remember one New Year's Eve—it was a Sunday, so our restaurant, La Grenouille, was closed and we decided to stay home. I said to my wife, "We're not going to go out and spend a fortune and be miserable." And she replied, "I want you to make scrambled eggs all night for me—that's all I want." So that's what we did. I brought back truffles and eggs—and, of course, a bottle of Krüg. They were showing a marathon of old Clint Eastwood movies on television. So we watched *Dirty Harry* all night and I made scrambled eggs and grilled bread with butter and salt, and added very thin shavings of truffle at the last moment. And it was heaven. It was heaven. We ate our eggs and drank our bottle of champagne, and it was simply the most perfect meal.

To this day, every time I cook a scrambled egg, I think of my father. What I learned from him about great cooking was this: choose from what's available and make the best with what you have right now.

Scrambled Eggs with Shaved Truffles

Serves 1

2 large farm-fresh eggs (use only
   1 yolk and 2 whites; if the yolks
   aren't bright orange, use 3
   whites and 2 yolks)

1 tablespoon whole milk

Pinch of flaky sea salt

4 teaspoons unsalted butter,
   softened

1 fresh black or white truffle, for
   shaving, or substitute chopped
   chives

ACCOMPANIMENT

Toasted baguette slices, buttered
   and sprinkled with flaky sea salt

1. Whisk the whites and yolk with the milk and salt so it becomes white and frothy, almost like a soufflé.

2. Take a pat of the butter on a piece of paper towel and glisten a small unheated cast-iron pan all over with it.

3. Put the pan over medium-high heat and, with another piece of paper towel, wipe the butter off so it doesn't burn. You just want the surface to shine.

4. When the pan is really, really hot, take it off the heat. Put 1 more pat of butter in the pan and let it dance all around and sizzle, and then wipe it off.

5. Add another pat of butter and when it stops sizzling, pour off the excess. Now the pan is the perfect temperature for the scrambled eggs.

6. Immediately add the egg mixture to the pan—off the fire. Mix it vigorously in the pan with a fork (you don't want any part of the egg to have a chance to stick) and then immediately flip it onto a warmed dish.

7. Fold the eggs, and using a truffle shaver or mandoline, top them generously with shaved truffle. Serve with slices of toasted baguette.

KIM CATTRALL
Actor

Meals, for this single woman, have taken on a new meaning. They aren't just fast fuel anymore. Eating a dry or soggy sandwich while rushing to a rehearsal, snacking off craft service on set, and inhaling protein bars washed down with caffeinated diet soda are all in my past.

Now taking the time to prepare and eat even the simplest of meals has become a source of deep satisfaction, whether I'm a guest, host, chef, or bottle washer. I'm practicing *essen*, not *fressen*. Life is too short to eat badly.

The ritual of planning, shopping, creating, preparing, and serving a meal no longer elicits panic or feels like a chore; rather it's a pleasure and a challenge. And not only when I'm cooking for guests, family, or a *inamorato de jour*, but simply just for myself. I now fearlessly attempt daunting new dishes I've always craved with the confidence of a pro, knowing that there is homemade pizza dough in the freezer, fresh mozzarella cheese in the fridge, and a can of whole tomatoes in the pantry should all crash and burn. It's a matter of preparation meeting inspiration and taking what any text gives you and making it your own.

Scrambled Eggs with Scallion and Turkey Bacon

Serves 1

1 tablespoon olive oil

1 scallion, trimmed and thinly sliced on the diagonal

1 slice turkey bacon, chopped

2 large eggs

Kosher salt and freshly ground black pepper

1 slice fresh country bread, toasted

This is my favorite breakfast for one.

1. Heat the oil in a small nonstick skillet over medium heat. Add the chopped scallion (reserve a few of the dark green slices for garnish if you like) and the turkey bacon and cook, stirring, until the scallion is softened, 2 to 3 minutes.

2. Whisk the eggs in a bowl and add to the skillet. Cook, stirring, until softly set, 1 to 2 minutes.

3. Remove from the heat, season with salt and pepper, and serve with toasted country bread.

GAIL SIMMONS
Food critic

When I was 18 years old, I had the fortuitous opportunity to spend the summer in Israel, working on a kibbutz in their chicken farm, gathering eggs. At first I despised the long hours, the monotonous work, and especially the thought of eating eggs for any reason (I felt nauseous anytime I even looked at one being cooked). It was difficult to associate my job, handling thousands of eggs and angry chickens each day, with what they were actually used for afterward. Over the course of the summer though, I began to realize just what a miracle the egg can be and what important work I was doing. Of course eggs are a symbol of life itself, but

the versatility of the humble egg as an ingredient in cooking and baking really cannot be matched. More than anything, they are incredibly nourishing and since that time have become my go-to meal, in a thousand shapes and forms, for breakfast, lunch, or dinner, whenever I'm feeling down or ill.

Harissa, the Middle Eastern chili paste, also is an ingredient I discovered that summer, and since then I've kept it in my fridge at all times. It's great in vinaigrettes, with grilled or roasted meat and vegetables, and especially with eggs; the deep roasted flavor combines just the right amount of heat with peppers and exotic spice. I love serving this dish of baked eggs with harissa as it reminds me so much of that time in my life. It also puts into perspective the important lesson I learned there: never to take for granted the complicated process by which fresh food comes from the farm to our table.

Baked Eggs with Harissa, Red Peppers, and Spinach

Serves 2

1 medium red bell pepper, stemmed, halved lengthwise, deveined and seeded

Extra-virgin olive oil

1 clove garlic, minced

6 ounces baby spinach

Kosher salt and freshly ground black pepper

4 to 6 large eggs

2 tablespoons heavy cream

1 tablespoon harissa (Moroccan hot red-pepper sauce)

2 ounces fresh goat cheese, crumbled

¼ teaspoon sweet paprika

1. Heat the broiler and put a rack in the upper third of the oven.

2. Line a small rimmed baking sheet with foil and put the peppers on top, cut sides down. Broil until well charred, 6 to 8 minutes. Transfer to a plastic bag to sweat 15 minutes, then peel and cut peppers crosswise into thin strips. Set aside.

3. Reduce the oven temperature to 375°F.

4. Set a 10-inch skillet over medium-high heat and add a drizzle of olive oil. Add the minced garlic and cook until slightly golden, about 1 minute. Add the spinach, a handful at a time, turning with tongs as you add more, and cook until all the spinach is wilted, 1 to 2 minutes total. Stir in the bell peppers and season with salt and pepper; then remove from heat. Drain mixture on paper towels to remove any excess moisture.

5. Oil 2 individual 8 by 4-inch gratin dishes and divide the spinach mixture between them. Make 2 or 3 "nestling spots" for eggs in each dish, and dab away excess moisture with paper towels. Gently crack an egg into each spot.

6. In a small bowl, stir together the cream and harissa. Drizzle the mixture over each dish; then drizzle with a little olive oil. Sprinkle evenly with pieces of goat cheese and season with the paprika.

7. Place the dishes on a rimmed baking sheet and bake in the upper third of the oven until the egg whites are cooked through but the yolks are still soft, about 6 minutes. Season eggs with salt and pepper and serve.

SOUPS
SALADS
&
SANDWICHES

DONNA KARAN
Fashion designer, philanthropist

To me, food is love. I'm sure it's the Jewish mother in me, but I must feed everyone around me. It doesn't matter what the context—family, friends, design, business—if there's a gathering of people, the first thing I will ask is, "What are we serving?" It can be a whole meal or as simple as raw cookies and fresh fruit. Only then can we talk. Or work. Or celebrate. Or sit around a table and laugh. The food gets it going.

I only serve healthy, natural food. I've been on a raw diet forever. It's how I lost a lot of weight, yes, but more important, it's how to get the most nutrition from food. So even if I'm not serving raw food—which isn't for everyone—I serve in the spirit of raw food: fresh ingredients, artfully prepared, seductively presented.

My obsession with healthy food became part of our Urban Zen wellness initiative, where we train and certify Urban Zen Integrative Therapists, who go into hospitals and homes to care for patients and caregivers alike. Because, while the medical world is worrying about the cure, someone needs to focus on the care. And that starts with the right nutrition. Yet it needs to taste good, otherwise who'd eat it?

When my husband Stephan was sick with lung cancer, there he'd be in the hospital, confined to a bed, trying to build strength and rally back after a treatment. And what did they bring him to eat? Something wholly unappetizing. So I started bringing Stephan my version of home cooking (I won't lie: we have a cook) starting with fresh juices and salads. I brought soups too, which is key, because they smell good. If there's ever a time you need something that smells good, it's when you're in the hospital. I also brought in what Stephan called my "woo woos": essential oils, yoga, massage therapy, acupuncture…anything that would make him feel better. And it did—especially the food.

By serving someone something that's delicious and nutritious, you're saying you're interested in their well-being. Food is a way to connect, communicate, collaborate, and most important, express how much you care. To me, food is love.

Forever-Green Salad with Creamy Basil Dressing

Serves 8

1 (¾-pound) bunch kale, ribs removed and leaves torn into bite-size pieces

4 ounces baby arugula (about 4 cups)

4 ounces baby spinach (about 4 cups)

1 green apple, diced

2 tablespoons sprouted pumpkin seeds or sunflower sprouts

CREAMY BASIL DRESSING

½ cup fresh basil leaves

3 tablespoons fresh lemon juice

1 tablespoon raw cashews

1 tablespoon freshly grated peeled ginger

1 medium clove garlic, peeled

1 teaspoon Celtic sea salt or kosher salt

½ cup extra-virgin olive oil

1. To make the dressing, put the basil, lemon juice, cashews, ginger, garlic, and salt in a blender along with 1 tablespoon of water; blend, slowly adding oil, until smooth. Season with more salt if needed.

2. Combine all the greens in a salad bowl. Add the apple and sprouts and toss with enough dressing to coat. Serve.

Editor's note: *Leftover dressing will keep in the refrigerator for up to one week.*

SIGOURNEY WEAVER

Actor

A few summers ago, my husband and I invited some of the wonderful young actors from his off-off-Broadway theater, the Flea, to rehearse a new A. R. Gurney play, *Office Hours*, up in the wilds of the Adirondacks. In mid-August, 12 members of the Bats (the official name of the company) appeared with sleeping bags and scripts. After rehearsing each day, the Bats and Jim would throw together wonderful

dinners, read old plays on the screened-in porch, and fall asleep in rustic lean-tos beside the lake to the cries of loons and the yips of coyotes.

It soon became clear that the wide spectrum of eating preferences in the group would be a challenge, since we were far from civilization. Jim had to make sure that what we cooked was appropriate and tasty for everyone.

Thank goodness our good friend Holly Chou was one of the 12 Bats. Holly is not only a gifted actor, but also a skilled and imaginative cook. After concocting delicious garlic chicken and ginger-glazed wild salmon for the group, Holly went online to see what else she could do with all the instant ramen noodles we had stored in the cupboard. She found and adapted this recipe for a delightfully refreshing and healthy salad, particularly good for family and friends who need a restorative and cheering meal. It's like a vacation in your mouth.

The salad is so popular that every year when we ask Holly to make it for our Christmas-caroling party, the next day my email is filled with requests for her recipe.

Napa Cabbage Salad with Ramen Crunchies

Serves 8 to 12 as a side dish or 6 as a main course

2 (3-ounce) packages instant ramen noodles (any flavor)

6 tablespoons (¾ stick) unsalted butter

1½ cups raw almonds, coarsely chopped

¼ cup sesame seeds

1 (2-pound) head napa cabbage

1 bunch scallions, thinly sliced, including green part

DRESSING

½ cup granulated sugar

6 tablespoons apple-cider vinegar

¼ cup soy sauce

¼ cup vegetable oil

1 teaspoon Asian sesame oil

1. Preheat the oven to 350° F.

2. Crush the ramen noodles inside their packages until broken up into small pieces. Open up the packages and discard the flavoring packets.

3. Melt the butter in a small skillet over medium-low heat. Put the broken-up ramen noodles, almonds, and sesame seeds on a large rimmed baking sheet, add the melted butter, and stir until everything is coated. Spread the mixture evenly and bake, stirring and turning the mixture often, until the crunchies are golden brown, 20 to 30 minutes. Transfer the baking sheet to a rack to cool completely.

4. Meanwhile, to make the dressing, combine the sugar, apple-cider vinegar, and soy sauce in a 2-quart saucepan and bring to a boil over medium-high heat, stirring until the sugar dissolves. Boil, uncovered, until the mixture is slightly syrupy, 3 to 4 minutes (you will have about ½ cup). Transfer to a medium bowl, whisk in the vegetable and sesame oils, and let cool to room temperature. Add salt if needed.

5. Quarter the cabbage lengthwise, core, and thinly slice crosswise. Put in a large salad bowl with the scallions.

6. Just before serving, add the crunchies and the dressing. Toss together and serve immediately.

Editor's note: *The cooled crunchies can be stored in an airtight container for 3 days.*

JIM BELUSHI

Actor, director, musician

When I was growing up, my father had a steakhouse in Chicago called Fair Oaks. It was named after a Civil War battle that took place on May 31 and June 1, 1862. Our whole family worked there: my mom, my dad, my sister Marian, my brother John, and myself. When you entered the restaurant, there was a display of antiquities from the Civil War: small revolvers, old photos, a rifle with a bayonet. The rest of the space was white tablecloths, beautiful chandeliers, red velvety wallpaper—a fine dining restaurant.

I begged my father to let me work there when I was 11 and he gave me the worst job to try to scare me off: dishwasher and pot cleaner. When he realized I loved it, he promoted me to busboy, along with John. John was a terrible busboy. I was a great busboy. He would put everything on me. I had to clear all the tables while he sat in the bathroom for hours on end. When I would say, "Hey John, what are you doing?" he would say, "Nothing." "That's right," I would reply. There would be a beat of silence, and then, through the bathroom door, he would say, "Shut up." He hated the restaurant. I loved it. If my father hadn't gone out of business in 1969, I would be serving dinner tonight. And, of course, John, thankfully, led me out of the restaurant business and into acting.

After I excelled at being a busboy, I was promoted to the pantry (while John sat on the toilet). This was a big deal. It was creative. Pantry was responsible for all the salads, appetizers, and relish trays that contained beet salad, bean salad, coleslaw, macaroni salad, egg salad—you get the idea. Everything was homemade. I was taught how to make all of those items from scratch. Fair Oaks was known for delicious steaks and seafood, but the real star of my dad's restaurant was the cream of garlic dressing. People came from Milwaukee and Rockford just for that dressing.

And one day, I earned it. I earned the right to make the cream of garlic dressing. Big, big deal. My cousin Ted took me downstairs—into the secret vault—where we made The Cream Of Garlic Dressing. The problem is that we made gallons and gallons and gallons of it. I cut more garlic than I've eaten in my lifetime and I think my fingers still smell. It was a combination of garlic, sour cream, and mayonnaise. The volume of ingredients is so overwhelming when you're making it in bulk that it was hard for me to modify it to a more responsible quantity. But here it is, thanks to my Uncle Dino, keeper of the recipe.

Cream of Garlic Dressing

Makes about 3 cups

2 cups mayonnaise

½ cup sour cream

½ cup ginger ale

¼ cup vegetable oil

2 tablespoons minced fresh garlic

1 teaspoon Worcestershire sauce

1 teaspoon kosher salt

Place all ingredients in a large mixing bowl and whip together. The dressing will keep for a week or two in a sealed container in the fridge.

HENRY WINKLER
Actor, children's book author

It's Thanksgiving. There is a table that stretches down the backyard of my house here in LA. It is decorated with pomegranates, persimmons, lemons, and limes, and the artwork that our three children created for the holiday from first grade on.

There are 60 chairs awaiting all our guests: family, our children's in-laws, friends, friends of friends, and lots of people who have no place to go.

There is another table piled high with sweet potatoes covered in marshmallows; asparagus soufflé, mashed potatoes, a moist turkey, biscuits, and two kinds of cranberry sauce—one with chunks, which I wouldn't even consider eating, and the other right out of the Ocean Spray can, which makes my turkey perfect.

The waiting is the hardest.

People arrive but we don't eat until 3pm. Not even football can distract me from pacing back and forth, waiting to fill my plate with my favorite meal of the year. Finally, it's time.

Ninety-nine percent of you who are reading this practice FHB (family holds back). Not me. If not the first, I'm the third in line at the buffet.

Once the table is filled up, we go around the table and everyone voices the most important thing they are thankful for. No one complains. Everyone loves hearing what everyone else has to say.

The thought of Thanksgiving, the feast, and the emotions shared on that holiday keeps me warm 365 days a year.

Here is a family recipe for a much-loved salad, which has also been a tradition in our house for more than 30 years. It is called simply the Mexican Salad. It adds the perfect complement to any meal, on any occasion, and it is my great pleasure to share it with you.

Mexican Salad

Serves 10 to 12

2 heads romaine lettuce, sliced crosswise at 1-inch intervals

¾ cup pitted Kalamata olives, sliced (or two 2-ounce cans sliced black olives)

1 pound ripe tomatoes (2 large), diced

1 large red onion, diced (2 cups)

½ pound sharp cheddar cheese, grated

1 (4-ounce) can diced green chilies

1 (6-ounce) bag tortilla or corn chips, coarsely crumbled

2 avocados, diced

DRESSING

¾ cup mayonnaise

½ cup green chile salsa or salsa verde

3 tablespoons ketchup

¼ teaspoon chili powder

1. Whisk together all ingredients for the dressing in a small bowl. Chill until ready to use.

2. Combine salad ingredients in a large bowl, adding chips and avocados just before serving.

3. Toss gently with chilled dressing and serve.

MICHAEL ANTHONY
Chef

In late October of 2011, I underwent open-heart surgery. There was no warning, no history of disease, no serious abuse that led the inner lining of my ascending aorta to tear. Sometimes things just break...

I was rushed to Beth Israel Hospital. There was very little time to spend with my wife, no chance to see my children, and no second option. Strange how a lifetime is ultimately translated into only minutes: clarified, distilled, precise, and yet unfair.

I woke up a day later with many questions swirling through my head. The immediacy of the surgery hadn't allowed me to contemplate what this might mean for my career as a chef. There had been more pressing issues at hand. Now that I had made it through and was starting to wrap my head around what happened, I wondered if my body—the body that had just betrayed me—would recover enough to allow me to return to the kitchen. I also wondered why this had happened to me. Why now? I have always felt proud of my diet and health-conscious cooking. I had led a balanced lifestyle, but still wondered if this condition was at all related to the way I had been eating.

After my surgery and homecoming, the gestures of encouragement poured in: get-well cards, concerned emails, thoughtfully chosen books and poems, inspirational movies, and carefully packed homemade meals. I appreciated everyone who reached out during this time, but it dawned on me that my fellow cooks had a special ability to connect and communicate through the food they shared. Some simply nourished and others dazzled, but every dish told a story. With the help of these restaurant folks and their deliveries, I eased my way back into being myself again by tasting each expression: barley and basil brought solidarity in tough times, kale-and-beet salad reconnected me with the garden, chicken fricassee invoked nostalgia, parsnip soup acted like a familiar handshake, poached lemon char sparked dreams, chocolate-chip cookies felt just like a pat on the back.

Each bite made me feel a profound sense of thanks to those who lent a hand or a meal when I needed it most. Their gestures pushed me to develop enough strength to return to the kitchen and reenter this dialog, and the generosity of spirit made me feel unbelievably proud to belong to the restaurant industry. Through careful choices and deliberate styles, informal gestures, and intricate work, whether immediately consumed or painstakingly preserved, we communicate so much with those who are at the receiving end of a thoughtful meal. While we work day in and day out to provide for our guests, my experience reminded me why taking care of one another comes first.

Sugar Snap Peas and Cucumbers

Serves 6

1 pound seedless Persian cucumbers, with peel, halved lengthwise and thinly sliced

Kosher salt

1 cup sugar snap peas, strings removed

1 tablespoon chopped fresh dill

1 tablespoon chopped fresh cilantro

1 tablespoon chopped fresh basil

1 teaspoon fresh lemon juice

1 tablespoon extra-virgin olive oil

1 cup cucumber dressing (see below)

CUCUMBER DRESSING

1 tablespoon olive oil

1 medium shallot, thinly sliced

1 clove garlic, thinly sliced

1 teaspoon wildflower honey

2 cups vegetable stock

1 pound seedless Persian cucumbers, peeled and thinly sliced

¼ cup mixed chopped fresh herbs, such as parsley, cilantro, and tarragon

½ ripe Hass avocado

3 tablespoons plain Greek yogurt

Kosher salt and freshly ground black pepper

1. To make the dressing, heat the oil in a 2-quart pot over medium-low heat and cook the shallot and garlic, stirring, until soft and translucent. Add the honey and allow to caramelize slightly. Add the vegetable stock and bring to a simmer. Add the cucumbers and simmer until slightly softened, about 10 minutes. Add the herbs and remove from heat.

2. Transfer the mixture to a medium metal bowl set over a larger bowl of ice and water and chill, stirring occasionally. When the vegetables are cold, strain them through a sieve set over a bowl, reserving vegetables and broth.

3. Blend the cucumber mixture in a blender with the avocado, yogurt, and enough of the broth to puree it to a smooth sauce. Strain the blended dressing through a fine-mesh strainer and season with salt and pepper. Chill, covered, until ready to serve the salad. (*The dressing can be made 1 day ahead.*)

4. To make the salad, begin by layering the sliced cucumbers, lightly salting them, in a colander set over a bowl. Let stand 20 minutes.

5. Bring a small pot of water to a boil. Boil the sugar snaps for 10 seconds and transfer to a bowl of ice water to stop the cooking. Drain the sugar snaps and thinly slice on the diagonal.

6. Rinse the cucumber slices and pat dry. Transfer them to a medium bowl and toss with the sugar snaps and chopped herbs. Drizzle with the lemon juice and olive oil and season with salt and pepper.

7. To serve, pour ¼ cup of the cucumber dressing into each of 4 wide soup dishes. Divide the salad equally among the dishes, mounding it in the center of the dressing.

ROZ CHAST
Cartoonist

MY DAD, WITH HIS FAVORITE FOODS

After my father retired, he ate these things for a kind of extended breakfast almost every day. These "smorgasbords," as he fondly referred to them, would begin at around 11 AM and end at 1 or 1:30 PM. He ate very slowly, partly because he didn't have good teeth, but mainly because he hated being rushed about anything. He was not a big guy. If anything, he was on the slight side. He died in 2007, at the age of 95.

I'm not much of a cook. I don't like to grocery shop, and I'm pretty lazy when it comes to food. I'd be happy to eat crackers and cheese, with a couple of glasses of wine – whatever's open – for dinner every night, if I didn't think that eventually I'd get rickets or all my hair would fall out. "That being said," here are a couple of easy, no-fail, inexpensive, and tasty things I make a lot:

ORZO SALAD –
great for pot lucks, block parties, etc. People seem to like it.

INGREDIENTS

- box of orzo, cooked & cooled
- chopped purple onion or scallions
- kalamata olives cut in half
- red pepper, chopped
- feta cheese, crumbled
- parsley, like a handful, chopped
- oil & vinegar to taste,
(or a basic bottled salad dressing, like Paul Newman's)

Combine everything in a large bowl. Toss, dress, serve.

Vegetable Soup
"You almost can't go wrong."

① In a large pot, sauté chopped onion, celery, and carrots in ± 2 tbsp. olive oil. Add a tablespoon or so of dried spices, like a mixture of basil, oregano, & thyme.
② When vegetables are soft, add about six cups of broth (or a combo of broth and water) and a can of diced tomatoes. Cook for about 5 min., then purée. ③ Add a handful of pearl barley or ½ c. of a dried small pasta. Cook till soft. ④ Add leftover chopped-up chicken or some sausage. ⑤ If you have parsley (fresh), chop & add.

SERVE WITH BREAD AND CHEESE, AND VOILÀ.

Orzo Salad

Serves 6 to 8

1 pound box orzo pasta

¼ cup white wine vinegar

1 teaspoon kosher salt, more for seasoning

½ teaspoon freshly ground black pepper, more for seasoning

½ cup extra-virgin olive oil

1 cup chopped red onion or scallions

½ cup Kalamata olives, pitted and halved

1 red bell pepper, diced

8 ounces feta cheese, crumbled

½ cup chopped fresh parsley

1. Cook the orzo in a pot of boiling salted water according to package directions until al dente. Reserve 1 cup of the pasta cooking water and drain.

2. Transfer the cooked orzo to a large bowl and toss with the vinegar, salt, pepper, and then the olive oil. Add the red onion or scallions, olives, bell pepper, feta, and parsley and toss to combine. Add more salt and pepper if needed. Serve warm or at room temperature.

Vegetable Soup

Serves 6 to 8

1 medium onion, chopped

1 medium carrot, chopped

1 large stalk celery, chopped

2 tablespoons olive oil, more for drizzling

1 teaspoon each dried basil, oregano, and thyme or 2 teaspoons each fresh

8 cups chicken broth (or a mixture of broth and water)

1 (14- to 15-ounce) can diced tomatoes

½ cup pearl barley or soup pasta

1 cup diced cooked chicken or sausage, optional

Kosher salt and freshly ground pepper

2 tablespoons chopped fresh parsley

ACCOMPANIMENTS

Crusty bread and finely grated Parmesan cheese

1. In a 4- to 5-quart pot over medium heat, cook the onion, carrot, and celery in the oil, stirring until softened, about 5 minutes. Add the dried herbs and cook, stirring, 1 minute. Add the broth and tomatoes, bring to a simmer, and simmer 5 minutes.

2. Carefully puree the soup in small batches in a blender and return to the pot. Return to simmer, add the barley or pasta, and cook, covered, until tender, about 45 minutes for the barley, or about 7 minutes for the pasta. Add the meat, if desired, to heat through, and season with salt and pepper. Garnish with the parsley and/or a drizzle of olive oil. Serve with Parmesan cheese and crusty bread on the side.

TRISHA YEARWOOD

Country singer, cookbook author, television host, lifestyle entrepreneur

I guess I've equated food with love ever since I was a little girl.
My mama was the best cook on the planet, and she had a homemade meal on the table every night when my daddy got home from work. Every night.

When we were sick, Mama would make us some form of chicken-noodle soup. It was the ultimate form of comfort, and she did this for as long as I can remember.

When I moved to Oklahoma in 2001, I was as far away from Georgia as I'd ever been in my life. I missed home a lot, and I missed my mama's cooking

as much as anything. My first winter in Oklahoma, I got the flu. I'm not a very good patient, as I'm hardly ever sick and I hate feeling under the weather. Now, I love my husband. He's my soul mate. He's the love of my life. But when I'm sick, nobody will do except Mama! Having the flu only made me more homesick for my family.

She must have sensed this, as good moms do, because the next day I got a package in the mail from Monticello, Georgia. It was Mama's chicken-noodle soup! She had made it for me, frozen it in quart containers, and shipped it overnight in a Styrofoam cooler. I was so happy I cried.

That was the best soup I'd ever eaten in my life. Not because it was the best soup she'd ever made, and not because I was sick, but because my mother knew how to show her love for me through that simple taste of home, even from hundreds of miles away. She wasn't there that day, but she was right there, you know?

My mom's gone now, so these kinds of memories are even more special. When I make her chicken-noodle soup now, I sense her here with me. That's the wonderful connection that comfort food brings. I still feel her love, passed down to me through these family recipes. They keep her alive for me, always.

Mama's Awesome Chicken-Noodle Soup

Adapted from *Georgia Cooking in an Oklahoma Kitchen* by Trisha Yearwood

Serves 10

1 (4-pound) hen or chicken

3 celery stalks with leafy tops, diced

3 carrots, diced

1 large sweet onion, such as Vidalia, diced

3 cloves garlic, thinly sliced

2 tablespoons kosher salt, more for seasoning

½ teaspoon freshly ground black pepper

½ teaspoon chopped fresh flat-leaf parsley

2 bay leaves

16 ounces frozen peas

8 ounces noodles, such as egg noodles or very thin spaghetti, broken into small pieces

1. Put the hen in a 10-quart stockpot and add water to cover, about 14 cups. Add the celery, carrots, onion, garlic, salt, pepper, parsley, and bay leaves. Bring to a boil over high heat, then immediately reduce the heat to a simmer. Skim off any foam that rises to the surface. Simmer the hen for 2 hours, or until the meat comes off the bone easily. Remove the hen to a large bowl and cool. Strain the broth into a large bowl and discard the vegetables. Let cool.

2. When the chicken is cool enough to handle, remove the meat from the bones, discarding the bones and skin, and shred the meat into bite-sized pieces. Chill in a bowl, covered, until ready to use.

3. If you have time, refrigerate the broth, uncovered, until cold, at least 4 hours. Skim off and discard any fat that has risen to the top. Otherwise, once the broth has settled, lay successive paper towels on top of the broth to absorb the fat, and discard.

4. Return the broth to a large pot. Add the shredded chicken, the frozen peas, and the noodles. Bring the soup to a boil, then simmer over medium heat for 10 minutes, or until the pasta is tender. Season with salt and serve.

LAURIE ANDERSON
Multimedia artist

In grade school my sister and I would race home from school and run into the kitchen.

We would make four peanut-butter sandwiches and pour two glasses of milk, and set them out on the kitchen counter with napkins.

Then we ran outside again, circled around and ran back into the kitchen.

"Wow! Look what Mom made for us!" we said. We each ate two sandwiches and drank the milk.

Picnic Peanut-Butter Sandwich

Spread peanut butter on two slices of fortified soft white bread. Combine pieces and slice in half diagonally.

Wrap in Saran wrap and pack in a brown bag with carrot sticks, an apple (Macintosh if possible) and a small box of raisins. Pack a thermos of cold milk. (*The empty raisin box is excellent for blowing into to create a small tune.*)

Toasted Peanut-Butter Sandwich

Toast 2 pieces of whole grain toast. While still hot, spread peanut butter on both slices. Make sure the toast is extra crisp. Slice in half diagonally. Serve with cold milk or a strawberry shake.

You can substitute almond butter or add iceberg lettuce for a crunchier sandwich.

JENNIFER HUDSON

Recording artist, actor, author

For me, cooking is all about being with the people I love. It's a social experience where we play music, catch up, and, at the end, enjoy a really nice meal together. My schedule is intense and I'm constantly traveling, so when I'm home, I cherish those moments most.

This recipe is one I always come back to; it's high in protein and full of amazing Mediterranean flavor. I don't cook often, so this is a relatively simple dish that's great for the summer. We love having friends and family over and grilling for everyone, and it's a nice change-up to the classic burger. You can also switch out the chicken for turkey if you want something even leaner, and sometimes I like to add cucumbers for a cool, crisp bite.

Feta-Stuffed Chicken Burgers

Serves 4

1 pound extra-lean ground chicken breast

1 tablespoon chopped fresh oregano

¼ teaspoon garlic powder

½ cup feta cheese, crumbled

4 pretzel-bread buns, halved horizontally

1 cup sliced romaine lettuce

⅔ cup sliced roasted red peppers

1. Prepare a grill for direct grilling or heat a broiler to high.

2. In a bowl, combine the chicken, oregano, garlic powder, and feta. Divide the mixture into 4 balls and press them gently into patties. Grill or broil the patties until the internal temperature registers 165°F on an instant-read thermometer, about 5 minutes on each side. Transfer to a plate and toast the buns briefly.

3. Serve the burgers in the buns with the lettuce and peppers.

Editor's note: *If you'd like a light and delicious dressing for these tender burgers, the Creamy Basil Dressing (page 39) makes a lovely accompaniment.*

APPETIZERS
VEGETABLES
&
SIDES

CHRISTOPHER IDONE

Cookbook author

My earliest childhood memory of the egg was the glass of milk that was mixed with a beaten egg and vanilla sugar, the weekly reward given to me and my brothers and sister for suffering through a nightly tablespoon of cod liver oil. But my appreciation of the true deliciousness of the egg came during a summer visit to my grandmother's house.

I could not have been older than five. I remember that each morning she would present me with a beat-up mushroom basket lined with a freshly pressed kitchen towel and send me out to the little red-painted pine shed. As I opened the door that creaked on rusty hinges, my eyes would adjust to the cool, dark room. What little light there was filtered down from a tiny window at the top of the eaves. I can still smell the shaved wood chips that came from the lumberyard a mile down the dirt road. Their smell was mixed with the pleasant scent of fresh-mown hay that my grandmother had placed in the individual cupboards stacked two tiers high off the floor of the shed. As I approached the coops, the chickens would flutter and scamper out of their nests and nervously scurry through the hatch to the wired pen behind. Gingerly, I'd remove the warm eggs one by one from the hay, delicately place them in the basket, close the shed door, and return to the kitchen.

By week's end I had become bold enough to clap my hands and shoo the stragglers out of their beds to retrieve their efforts. The eggs were pale in color, not quite white but cream colored. Some were shades of tan or beige, some freckled with brown spots, and a few were pale blue. The water was already simmering when I returned with my basket and my grandmother would wash the eggs and set them into the water, one for each of us, and in three and a half minutes they would be done. She would place them in porcelain eggcups, pick up a knife and lightly tap off the tops. Then she would season them with a little salt and pepper and offer me a small silver spoon and a plate of buttered toast, the crusts removed and sliced in long fingers we called soldiers. They were just right to reach the golden yolk, as bright and orange as a rising sun.

Deviled Eggs

Makes 20

1 dozen large eggs

¼ cup homemade mayonnaise (see below)

1 tablespoon Creole mustard

½ teaspoon minced fresh tarragon

1 tablespoon unsalted butter, softened

Kosher salt and freshly ground black pepper

Finely chopped fresh chives for garnish

MAYONNAISE (makes about 1 cup)

2 large egg yolks, at room temperature

1 tablespoon fresh lemon juice

½ teaspoon Dijon mustard

¼ teaspoon kosher salt

⅛ teaspoon freshly ground white pepper

Dash of cayenne pepper

⅓ cup olive oil and ⅓ cup vegetable oil

1 to 2 tablespoons boiling water

1. To make the mayonnaise, place the yolks, lemon juice, mustard, salt, pepper, and cayenne in the bowl of a food processor or standing mixer. Process or beat until combined. While the motor is running, slowly add all the oil in a thin stream. Add 1 tablespoon of the boiling water and process or beat for a few seconds. Add more boiling water if the mixture needs to be looser. Adjust the seasoning. If not using all the mayonnaise right away, keep chilled in an airtight container.

2. Put the eggs in a large pot with cold water to cover. Bring to a boil, reduce the heat to a simmer, and cook 12 minutes. Set the pot in the sink under cold running water and crack the shells while the water is cooling the eggs. When the eggs are cool to the touch, peel under the water.

3. Halve the eggs lengthwise, remove the yolks, and put them in a medium bowl. Add the remaining ingredients and mix well with a fork. Put in a pastry bag fitted with a plain tip (or use a spoon) and fill 20 of the whites. (Discard the remaining 4 whites or reserve for another use.) To serve, arrange on a platter and garnish with chives.

DAVID SALLE
Artist

The arrival at the farm stand of fava beans—big heaps of soft yellow-green pods—is one of the most reliably pleasurable markers of early summer. For some reason, not many farmers grow them; they show up at only a few of the places I frequent. Pike's farm stand in Sagaponack, Long Island, on Sagg Main Street just south of the highway, has a few wooden tubs of favas for a couple of weeks in early or mid-June. Maralee Foster, whose stand, which is called "Heuristics" and is just down the road from Pike's, will also have a few handfuls from time to time. In both cases, you have to get there early.

When very young and tender, the beans can be eaten raw, often accompanied by a sharp pecorino cheese, along with a glass of a fresh, light red wine. Turning favas into a puree is a little bit of work, but the resulting depth of flavor—its balance of earthiness and bright fruitiness—rewards the effort.

Fava-Bean Puree

Makes 2 cups

2 pounds fresh fava beans in their pods, shelled (about 2 cups)

3 medium and 1 small cloves garlic

1 tablespoon fresh lemon juice

¾ teaspoon kosher salt

¾ teaspoon freshly ground black pepper

¼ cup best-quality extra-virgin olive oil

Thick-sliced sourdough bread

1. Put the shelled fava beans in a pot of boiling water for 1 minute, drain, and cool in a bowl of ice water. Drain. Remove and discard the skins. (You can usually make a small slit in the bottom of the membrane with your thumbnail, after which the skin slips off easily.)

2. Bring a saucepan of water to a boil. Thinly slice 2 of the medium garlic cloves and add to the pot along with the skinned favas. Boil until the favas are tender, 3 to 5 minutes. Reserve ½ cup of the cooking water and drain.

3. Put the favas (and cooked sliced garlic) in a food processor with ¼ cup of the cooking liquid. Mince the small clove of garlic and add to the processor along with the lemon juice, salt, and pepper. Puree, slowly pouring the olive oil through the feed tube. If it's very stiff, add a little more of the cooking water. Add more lemon juice, salt, and pepper to taste.

4. Prepare a medium-hot grill or heat a griddle over medium-high heat.

5. Cut the remaining medium clove of garlic in half and rub the bread slices with it. Grill the bread to your liking and serve with the fava-bean puree.

Editor's note: *The fava-bean puree will keep for 3 days in the fridge. Bring to room temperature before serving.*

TONY MAY
Restaurateur

When I was growing up in Italy, my mother was so busy raising eight kids that she could not—and still cannot at the tender age of 96—find time to boil water! But I never had a bad meal in my childhood home. My grandmother did all the cooking at first; then it was my aunt, and finally my father, when he retired. I learned a bit from each of them, but what they taught me most of all was how important it was to start with the right ingredients. Many times they would travel some distance to a neighboring town just to find a particular product to make a dish just right.

When I came to America from Italy I found a country whose version of Italian food was completely unlike the dishes and flavors I knew. While I was already a culinary professional when I arrived, I made a promise to myself to change this misperception. I dedicated myself, body and soul, to becoming successful enough to be able to influence and alter the American image of Italian cuisine. I do not believe I achieved it … but I made a dent!

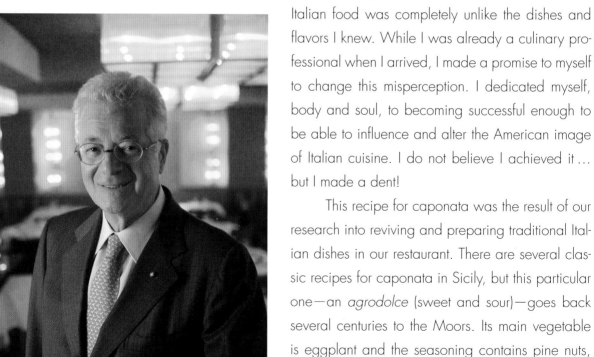

This recipe for caponata was the result of our research into reviving and preparing traditional Italian dishes in our restaurant. There are several classic recipes for caponata in Sicily, but this particular one—an *agrodolce* (sweet and sour)—goes back several centuries to the Moors. Its main vegetable is eggplant and the seasoning contains pine nuts, raisins, a touch of sugar, and wine vinegar. It not only caught our attention, but also the attention of our customers, quickly becoming one of our most popular items—and a staple on the menu.

In my perfect world, the ideal setting for this meal would be a warm summer night at a restaurant in Capri with a view of Marina Piccola and the moon shining perfectly between the two *faraglioni*—the enormous rock formations that rise up majestically from the sea just off the island's coast. The dinner would be prepared by Chef Odette Fada, the best Italian cook I know of in America, and the company would be only those friends who share my desire and longing for the simple pleasure of a great dining experience.

Eggplant Caponata

Serves 6

2 medium eggplants (2 pounds total), skin on, cut into 1-inch cubes

Kosher salt

½ cup golden raisins

½ cup extra-virgin olive oil, more as needed

½ cup chopped onion

3 medium cloves garlic, chopped

¼ cup white wine vinegar

2 celery stalks, diced

6 anchovy fillets, chopped

1 (15-ounce) can whole plum tomatoes in juice

2 ounces green olives, pitted and halved lengthwise (scant ½ cup)

Freshly ground black pepper

Chopped parsley and mint leaves, for garnish

ACCOMPANIMENT

Grilled bread or crostini

1. Arrange the eggplant cubes in layers in a colander set over a plate, sprinkling each layer lightly with salt (about 1½ teaspoons total) and let stand 45 minutes.

2. Bring 1 cup water to a boil in a small saucepan and add the raisins. Turn off the heat and let stand 20 minutes to soften. Drain.

3. Heat 2 tablespoons of the olive oil in a large skillet over medium heat, add the onions and garlic, and cook, stirring, until the onions are softened, about 5 minutes. Add the vinegar and boil 1 minute. Add the celery, anchovies, and tomatoes, including juice, and simmer for 10 minutes, breaking up the tomatoes with the side of the spoon. Add the drained raisins and the olives. Transfer to a large bowl to cool.

4. Squeeze the eggplant dry in your hands.

5. In the cleaned skillet over medium-high heat, heat 3 tablespoons of the remaining olive oil until shimmering hot. Add half of the eggplant and fry, turning with tongs, until tender and browned, about 10 minutes. Transfer the eggplant to paper towels to drain and repeat with the remaining olive oil and eggplant.

6. Add the eggplant to the tomato mixture and toss gently to combine. Season with salt and pepper. Transfer to a serving dish and garnish with chopped parsley and mint leaves. Serve with grilled bread or crostini.

Editor's note: *Caponata will keep, refrigerated, for up to a week. Bring to room temperature before serving.*

LUCY LIU

Actor

When I traveled to Africa for safari years ago, I had a beautiful experience learning about the land and the animals. After a long day of adventures, we would all sit down together and eat a gorgeous meal that was just food from the earth, prepared with simplicity. Roasted vegetables and grains never tasted so good. That's when I learned to enjoy eating vegetables just as nature intended. A little olive oil and salt and *voilà*! I brought this idea to my dear friend Melissa, who is a chef, and we came up with this very clean and delicious dish that we love sharing with all our friends and family.

My friendship with Melissa grew over our mutual love of food and our similar approach to cooking. Our formula is simple: the best seasonal ingredients + easy preparation + love + balance = a perfect meal. We call our dish the Planet Platter. It's basically a mix of grains and vegetables, roasted to perfection and served with simple, flavorful dressings. I like to try different combinations depending on the time of year.

Here is our favorite platter with two dressings: one that's lighter for spring/summer, and one for fall/winter to warm your soul. All of the components are healthful and nutritious. Melissa and I love to leave the skins on both the yam and the kabocha squash to increase our fiber intake. Other veggies that could be added or used instead of the ones we've included are zucchini, asparagus, beets, seaweed—or whatever you love the most. Happy eating!

Planet Platter with Two Dressings

Serves 4 to 6

2 medium yams (6 to 8 ounces each), rinsed

1 (1 to 1½ pounds) delicata squash with peel, rinsed

3 teaspoons olive oil

1 teaspoon fine sea salt

1 cup quinoa

2 cups vegetable broth or water

2 daikon radishes (about 8 ounces each), peeled

2 bunches broccolini, coarse ends trimmed, if necessary, and rinsed

SESAME-BRAGG'S DRESSING

3 tablespoons fresh lemon juice

¼ cup Bragg's liquid aminos

1 tablespoon Asian sesame oil

2 tablespoons extra-virgin olive oil

CARROT-GINGER-TAHINI DRESSING

2 large organic carrots, peeled and coarsely grated (about 1 cup)

1- to 2-inch piece of fresh ginger root, peeled and thinly sliced

¼ cup Bragg's liquid aminos

2 tablespoons rice vinegar

2 tablespoons tahini

1. To make the sesame-Bragg's dressing, whisk together all ingredients in a small bowl. To make the carrot-ginger-tahini dressing, combine all ingredients in a blender and blend until smooth and creamy.

2. Preheat the oven to 400°F. Line two baking sheets with foil and set aside.

3. Prick the yams with a fork or knife and roast on a rack in the oven until tender, about 1 hour.

4. Cut the delicata squash in half, remove the seeds, and cut the halves crosswise into 1-inch sections. In a large bowl, toss the squash with 1 teaspoon of the olive oil and ¼ teaspoon of the sea salt. Arrange on one of the prepared baking sheets (you can add the yams to the baking sheet at this point) and roast for 30 minutes.

5. In a medium saucepan, combine the quinoa, vegetable broth or water, 1 teaspoon of the olive oil, and ½ teaspoon of the sea salt. Bring to a boil over medium-high heat, then turn the heat to low, cover, and cook for 15 minutes. Turn off the heat, keep covered, and let steam for 5 minutes to finish cooking.

6. Halve the daikon radishes lengthwise and then cut halves crosswise into 1-inch sections. Put the radishes in a saucepan with cold water to cover and bring to a boil. Boil until tender, about 10 minutes.

7. In a large bowl, toss the broccolini with the remaining teaspoon of olive oil and ¼ teaspoon sea salt. Arrange in a single layer on the second prepared baking sheet. Roast until browned and crispy, 10 to 12 minutes.

8. Peel the yams and cut into large wedges. Arrange all the vegetables and the quinoa in piles on a platter and put the two dressings in serving bowls.

MERYL STREEP

Actor

Sometimes cooking is celebratory; sometimes it is the thing we offer to others as tangible help in times of distress. This is a recipe adapted from a dish my friend Joe Grifasi brought to a supper of close friends after a loss, and it brought us soft comfort together around a table.

I can attest that it serves well on happier occasions as well, as its roots, like Joe's, are in Sicily, where laughter and tears mingle freely, and the best thing is to feel all that life can bring, deeply.

This dish can start out hot and sit happily through the hours of a long evening; the taste just deepens as it cools to lukewarm, and people will keep going back for just a little more.

Veggies from the Bottom of the Boot

Serves 6 to 8

1 large eggplant, cut into 1-inch cubes

1 tablespoon kosher salt, more for seasoning

½ head cauliflower, cut into bite-size florets

3 large leeks, white and light green parts quartered lengthwise and rinsed well, then strips halved crosswise

1 cup extra-virgin olive oil

Freshly ground black pepper

10 anchovy fillets

10 medium cloves garlic, peeled and thinly sliced lengthwise

This recipe can be served as a side dish, a vegan main dish (without the Parmesan and anchovies), or over pasta.

1. Preheat the oven to 450°F.

2. Put the eggplant cubes into a colander set over a bowl, toss with 1 tablespoon of salt, and let stand 20 minutes.

3. Put the cauliflower florets in a steamer and steam, covered, until crisp tender, 3 to 4 minutes.

4. Spread the leek strips on a large rimmed baking sheet, drizzle with about 2 tablespoons of the olive oil and sprinkle with salt and pepper.

5. Put the eggplant cubes on another large rimmed baking sheet, toss with ½ cup of the olive oil and spread in a single layer.

¼ teaspoon dried red pepper flakes

½ cup Sicilian green olives, pitted and halved

½ cup Cerignola or Kalamata olives, pitted and halved

1 teaspoon chopped fresh thyme

½ cup lightly toasted pine nuts

1½ cups basil leaves, torn

1 small lemon, halved and seeded

Chunk of Parmigiano-Reggiano for shaving, optional

6. Roast the eggplant and leeks in the oven until the leeks become limp and almost crisp at the edges, and the eggplant cubes are softened and browned (turn occasionally so they brown evenly), 20 to 30 minutes.

7. Meanwhile, put the anchovies and ⅓ cup of the olive oil in a large skillet over medium heat. Cook, stirring with a fork until the anchovies have disintegrated. Add the garlic and red pepper flakes and cook, stirring, until the garlic starts to brown. Add the olives, cauliflower, and thyme and stir to coat with the oil. Add the eggplant and leeks and stir to heat through. Remove from the heat. Stir in the pine nuts and basil, and season with salt and pepper.

8. Transfer to a large serving dish, drizzle with the remaining tablespoon or so of olive oil, and squeeze the lemon over the top. Shave some of the Parmigiano-Reggiano, if desired, over all and serve.

NONA HENDRYX

Music artist

My mother, Nona B, was 73 years of age when she opened her own soul-food restaurant on the edge of Trenton, New Jersey.
The oldest of seven sisters and seven brothers, with seven children of her own, my mother found cooking as easy as breathing. I rarely saw a measuring cup or spoon in her hands; recipes were measured by the eye, and shared or learned by doing. She didn't have time to write down recipes, she was too busy being a mother, grandmother, great-grandmother, and provider. When she first moved to New Jersey, she cleaned houses; then she raised children of the wealthy, co-owned a hair salon with a friend, and organized an office-cleaning service. She eventually retired from a lifetime of hard work, which had begun in her child-hood in the fields of Sylvania, Georgia, helping her parents farm their land. But

having spent most of her 73 years constantly cooking, cleaning, and looking after others, she didn't allow her retirement to last long. My brother gave her a poodle and someone else gave her a Siamese cat; she loved them both but they didn't fulfill her. My mother missed her interaction with people, community, food, and being busy. Soon, Nona B's was opened!

It was a small restaurant space, one street from the bungalow my mother had moved into after selling her larger house, also one street away. There was a counter, room for three or four tables, a soft-drink cooler, several deep fryers, and a large commercial stove with two ovens. In the beginning the menu was whatever she decided the night before or even on the day. That changed when more people heard about Nona B's and began to ask her to include more traditional soul-food dishes on the menu.

The dish many of her generation couldn't find anywhere else was stewed or fried chitterlings (pig intestines). My mother would buy them on Wednesday, and clean, cook, and add them to the menu on Thursday and Friday. Some people would either call on Tuesday or Wednesday to secure their order ahead of time or line up at the restaurant on Chitterlings' Day. Other favorites were her nongreasy fried chicken (an art), deviled eggs, candied yams, potato salad, slow-cooked string beans with fatback bacon, collard greens with turkey meat, neck-bone stew, beef stew, lima beans and rice, black-eyed peas, smothered pork chops, meat loaf, porgies, and her delicious, tasty, and filling tomato stew served over rice or pasta.

She also baked her own pastries and breads: moist and fluffy biscuits, corn bread, muffins, bread loaves, and piecrusts. She made bread pudding, banana pudding, peach and blueberry cobblers; a variety of pies—sweet potato, pumpkin, apple, peach; and cakes of all kinds—chocolate layer, vanilla layer, pineapple upside down, coconut, strawberry shortcake—I'm getting hungry as I write!

My mother's retirement problem was solved; people came for breakfast, lunch, and dinner. The only time Nona B's was closed was on Sunday, her day of rest: she went to church to do her missionary work, which sometimes included cooking!

Nona B's Tomato Stew

Makes about 5 quarts

4 medium waxy potatoes

6 freshly picked ears of corn, shucked

8 pounds ripe red tomatoes, cored and with X's cut through skin on opposite ends

1½ pounds okra, cut crosswise into ½-inch pieces

6 stalks celery, cut crosswise into ½-inch slices

1 onion, chopped

1 small clove garlic, minced

2 tablespoons kosher salt

1 tablespoon freshly ground black pepper

This recipe yields an amount appropriate for canning (quart-sized Mason jars are what my mother used). Or you can simply halve or quarter the recipe if you wish to eat it fresh.

1. Put the potatoes in a 3- to 4-quart pot and fill with cold water. Bring to a boil, covered, and boil until the potatoes are just cooked through (pierce with a paring knife). Transfer the potatoes with a slotted spoon to a cutting board. Add the corn to the boiling water and cook 3 minutes. Transfer to the cutting board with the potatoes. Keep the water boiling.

2. While the potatoes and corn cool slightly, lower the tomatoes, 2 or 3 at a time, into the boiling water for 15 to 30 seconds (cut skin will loosen), and transfer with the slotted spoon to a very large bowl of cold water to stop cooking. Peel the tomatoes, halve them crosswise, and dig out seeds with your finger. Put the pulpy seeds in a strainer set over a bowl and press to extract all the juices. Discard the seeds. Coarsely chop the tomatoes and add them to the bowl, along with any juices from chopping. Place in a heavy nonreactive 10- to 12-quart pot (or divide between 2 smaller pots).

3. Peel the potatoes and cut into small pieces. Stand the ears of corn, one at a time, in a wide bowl and cut the kernels off with a sharp knife. Discard the cobs.

4. Add the potatoes, corn, okra, celery, onion, and garlic to the pot. Add the salt and pepper and stir. Cover and bring to a simmer over medium heat, stirring frequently to avoid burning on the bottom. Continue until the celery is just tender, 30 to 45 minutes from the time you turned the heat on.

5. Let stand 15 to 20 minutes and serve.

DAN KLUGER
Chef

Food to me is far more than just sustenance. Every meal is an opportunity to replenish, to find comfort, to come together with friends, new or old, to share stories, laughter, and memories—and as a chef, to show my love through what I put on the plate.

I started "cooking" when I was very young, just helping my parents at home on the weekends or spending time at my friend's bakery on Manhattan's Upper West Side (when I was nine years old, I was going in at 7am to make croissants with the owner!). Later, in college, I started to develop a serious inter-

est in the restaurant/food-service industry. I took a basic food-science class, which I immediately loved, and it soon became clear that I had found my passion. After graduating, I went to work as a host in the dining room at Union Square Café, where I'd done a summer externship as an undergrad. I spent my days off in the kitchen watching and learning so that one day, when I became a dining-room manager, I would have a better understanding of the back of the house. That ended up leading to a job as a prep cook, and I continued to work my way up through the USC kitchen. Eventually, I left to open Tabla with Chef Floyd Cardoz. It was around this time that things really started to click and I began to find my own "voice" as a chef.

Floyd taught me so much about flavors, textures, and truly cooking from the heart. He was also a big supporter of the greenmarket, and it was while working with him that I began to forge

collaborative relationships with local farmers, many of whom I still work with today. Seven years later I joined Tom Colicchio on a private club project. There I was able to put my season- and flavor-driven food to the test. It was also the first time I really had the opportunity to see how my cooking could directly uplift those I served. Seeing the impact I was making on customers started to feed my soul as I fed theirs. Over the next decade I continued honing my skills—and had the amazing opportunity to work with Jean-Georges on the ABC projects, and more.

I love making people happy with good food and am still always search-ing out new inspirations and ideas to try out in the kitchen and share with my restaurant guests. Many days, I feel like I've won the lottery with this job. I can't imagine doing anything more rewarding—or creative—than cooking for others.

Roasted Butternut Squash with Spicy Granola

Serves 4 for breakfast or as a side dish

3 tablespoons extra-virgin olive oil, preferably Arbequina

1 (2-pound) butternut squash, halved and seeded

2 teaspoons kosher salt

½ teaspoon freshly ground black pepper

½ cup organic Greek yogurt

1 tablespoon finely chopped fresh rosemary*

1 recipe granola (see below)

2 tablespoons coarsely chopped fresh mint

*Chop the rosemary finely, but only cut through it one time.

GRANOLA

¼ cup old-fashioned rolled oats

1 tablespoon raw hulled pumpkin seeds

1 tablespoon cashews, coarsely chopped

1 tablespoon sliced almonds

2 tablespoons pure maple syrup

1 tablespoon extra-virgin olive oil, preferably Arbequina

2 teaspoons light brown sugar

⅛ teaspoon ground cinnamon

⅛ teaspoon smoked paprika

Pinch of red pepper flakes

¾ teaspoon kosher salt

1 tablespoon golden raisins

1 tablespoon dried sour cherries

2 teaspoons finely chopped candied ginger

1. To make the granola, preheat the oven to 325°F (300°F if you have a convection oven).

2. Put the oats, pumpkin seeds, nuts, syrup, olive oil, brown sugar, spices, and ½ teaspoon of the salt in a large bowl and mix well. Spread the mixture evenly on a small rimmed baking sheet lined with a silicone sheet or parchment paper. Bake, stirring every 10 minutes, until the granola is golden brown, about 25 minutes.

3. Transfer the pan to a rack, sprinkle with the remaining ¼ teaspoon of salt, and scatter the raisins, dried cherries, and ginger on top. When cool, toss well to combine, breaking up any big clumps.

4. To prepare the squash, preheat the oven to 375°F.

5. Drizzle 1 tablespoon of the olive oil over the squash, rub it into the flesh, and season with a teaspoon of the kosher salt and with the pepper. Put the squash, cut side down, on a rimmed baking sheet and roast until tender, about 45 minutes. Transfer the pan to a rack and let the squash sit until it's cool enough to handle.

6. Scoop the flesh into a bowl and discard the skins. Add the yogurt, rosemary, and remaining teaspoon of kosher salt and toss until combined but with the squash still a bit chunky.

7. To serve, put the squash mixture (after reheating in oven if necessary) in a serving bowl. Drizzle with the remaining 2 teaspoons of olive oil and add more salt if needed. Sprinkle generously with the granola and top with the chopped mint.

BRENT RIDGE & JOSH KILMER PURCELL

Farmers, authors, television personalities, entrepreneurs

Both Josh and I grew up in rural environments. Our families had to garden because that's what put food on the table. A lot of the recipes in our cookbooks are adaptations of family recipes—dishes we watched our grandmothers, aunts, and mothers make—which we've modernized. What we believe, and try to share with people, is that if you're eating really good, well-prepared food, even if it happens to be fried, and you're not using anything artificial or chemically influenced, that you feel more satiated. So you actually eat less.

We cook dinner every night we are home and each meal is somehow inspired by the farm, because we raise or grow about 80 percent of all the food

we personally consume. Most people come home, open up the pantry and say, what do I want to make? It is the exact same process for us, except we walk out to the garden and see what needs to be harvested. And then we bring it into the kitchen and say, "Okay, what can we do with this?" We're just shopping the garden.

For me, relaxing is having my hands in the dirt, working in the yard or the flower garden. For Josh, it's cooking. He comes in at the end of the day and sorts everything out in his head while he prepares dinner. It's how he processes his day.

As founders of the Beekman 1802 brand, the two of us are together 24/7, literally. We get up together. We go to work together. We're out tending the farm together. But it doesn't become overwhelming, because work is our life. And life is our work. It's almost seamless. We're always excited by what we're doing—neither one

of us ever wakes up thinking, "I don't want to have to go to work today." Because we have found what we're passionate about.

Our fennel recipe is a twist on a dish Josh used to make with his mom. We were doing a book signing in North Carolina and we saw the owners of this small root beer company doing a cooking demo. They were a mom-and-pop operation, harvesting the roots, and making the beer themselves. We tasted it and loved it. We said to them, "We want to come up with a recipe that we can put on our website and link back to yours, so that people buy your root beer." And so, that's how we took Josh's family's fennel recipe and combined it with root beer to create something completely new and modern.

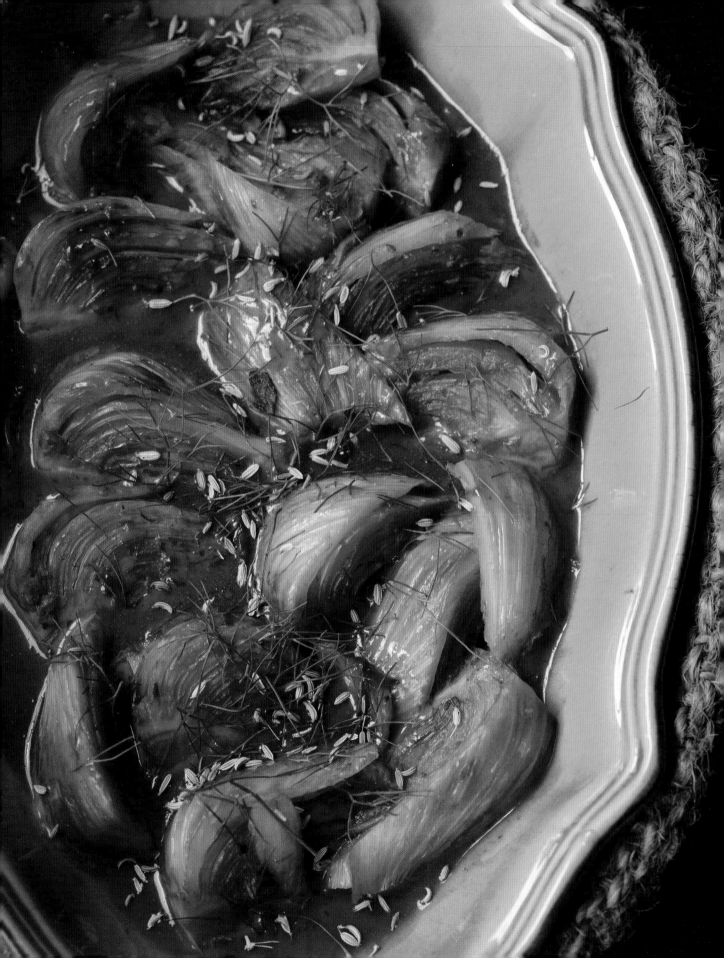

Root Beer Fennel

Serves 4

1½ teaspoons fennel seeds

3 tablespoons olive oil

2 cloves garlic, peeled and smashed

2 large fennel bulbs (about 3 pounds total), stalks removed (reserve fennel fronds), each bulb cut into 8 wedges

1 (12-ounce) bottle good-quality root beer (1½ cups)

Pinch of kosher salt, more for seasoning

2 cups chicken or vegetable stock, or as needed

¼ cup heavy cream

Freshly ground black pepper

2 tablespoons chopped or picked fennel fronds

1. Heat the fennel seeds in a 12-inch heavy skillet over medium heat, stirring frequently, until lightly toasted, 2 to 3 minutes. Be careful not to burn. Transfer seeds to a small bowl.

2. Add the olive oil and garlic to the skillet and heat over medium-high heat. Add the fennel wedges and cook, turning occasionally, until browned on all sides, 5 to 8 minutes total. Add the root beer and salt, and gently stir to deglaze the pan. Add the stock and bring to a simmer. Turn the heat to low, cover the skillet, and gently simmer for 20 to 25 minutes, until the fennel is tender.

3. Transfer the fennel wedges to a serving platter. Raise the heat to high, and boil the liquid until reduced by half (about 1 cup). Stir in the heavy cream and season with salt and pepper. Remove from the heat.

4. Pour the sauce over the fennel, garnish with the toasted fennel seeds and the fronds, and serve immediately

TAMAR ADLER

Writer

It seems to me that everyone about whom it has been said "she could not even boil water" should have been more rightly accused of not wanting to. We said of my father often that he *could* not, when it was really that he *would* not. He was good with his hands, good with his mind, but he would not boil water for tea—never mind for pasta—or heat a pan for toasted cheese sandwiches ... until one evening when I was eight years old or so. On that memorable night, he was inspired to replicate the thinly sliced rosemary roasted potatoes that were a favorite of ours, often made by our mother for Friday dinner.

It was strange to see him there in the kitchen, strange to see him holding a knife, opening an oven door. Stranger still when the potatoes emerged, crackly crisp in places, perfectly cooked everywhere, an expert specimen. We reported the success to our mother—who had been out—who was as shocked as we were and relieved that finally our father was ready to take up his part of the cooking burden.

It was not to be. That was the only time he ever made the potatoes, and he remained unwilling to make tea. He argued, repeatedly and illogically, that he did not know how to do either, and no amount of evidence to the contrary would get him to change his tune. A greater injustice is that, even though he only made them once, I've ever since thought of these potatoes as *his*, proving, certainly, something about the unfair value of novelty.

Rosemary and Butter Roasted Potatoes à la David Adler

Serves 4

1 pound fingerling potatoes, sliced into ¼-inch rounds

2 ounces (½ stick) unsalted butter

1 tablespoon chopped fresh rosemary

½ teaspoon kosher salt

1. Preheat the oven to 425°F.

2. Melt the butter in a small pan and add the rosemary.

3. Coat the bottom of a shallow 9 by 13-inch baking dish or small rimmed baking sheet with half the rosemary butter. Lay the potatoes in slightly overlapping rows in a single layer. Drizzle with the remaining butter. Sprinkle evenly with the salt.

4. Bake until the potatoes are tender and beginning to crisp, about 30 minutes. Serve.

ALAN CUMMING

Actor

I met Karen Black in the bar of the Chateau Marmont in Los Angeles in 2005. I was directing a film and I wanted her to play a part in it. We moved around to three different sofas until the lighting was to her liking and immediately I fell in love with her. The part was not written for a woman of her age but I just knew that she would be amazing in it, and she was. She was the kindest, funniest, kookiest, least selfish person I've ever met. She died after a long battle with cancer, and her husband asked me to sing at her memorial. I chose one of her own compositions and it was such a great feeling to be channeling Karen and making everyone laugh that day. If you want to sing this song, it's basically a traditional blues riff, so just give it a go. She'll be delighted to hear you.

I woke up in the morning
Seemed like the middle of the night
I looked around my room
Not a piece of cake in sight
My boyfriend the doctor
He left me sad and blue
But I won't slit my wrists
Cos I know exactly what to do

I'm gonna drown my troubles
In a Big Mac chocolate shake
I'm gonna swallow my pride
With a Sara Lee fudge cake

I'm gonna be too big to cry
And too fat to get down

I'm gonna quell my longing with what really satisfies—
burrito chili dog and fries

I'm gonna be too big to cry
And too fat to get down

Yumyumyum
This is love that money CAN buy
You get what you see
This is love that never lies
Ronnie McDonald
You're my kind of clown
Bobby big boy
You're MY big boy now

I'm gonna be too big to cry
And too fat to ever
Too big to cry
And too fat to ever
Too big to cry
And too fat to get
Down!

Stovies

Serves 6 as a main course or 12 as a side dish

¼ cup olive oil

4 cloves garlic, chopped

4 large onions, very coarsely chopped (about 2 pounds total)

8 to 10 medium–large Yukon Gold potatoes (about 4 pounds total), scrubbed and cut into 1-inch pieces

2 teaspoons kosher salt

1 teaspoon freshly ground black pepper

2 tablespoons tamari (aged soy sauce), more if desired

2 tablespoons Worcestershire sauce, more if desired

⅓ cup textured vegetable protein (TVP), more if desired

Stovies are real peasant food, and ideal for people who, like me, enjoy a big plateful of one thing.

1. Put a good splash of olive oil into a wok or wide 6- to 7-quart pot over medium heat. Add the garlic and stir-fry until pale golden. Add the onions, stir-fry for a minute, and then cover the pot and let the onions sweat for 5 minutes. Add the potatoes to the onions and garlic and cook over low heat, stirring occasionally, to infuse the flavors, about 5 minutes.

2. Add the salt and pepper, tamari, and Worcestershire sauce to the wok. Throw in the textured vegetable protein. It swells up in the water and gives the stovies nice texture and taste and also makes them thicker. Pour water into the wok so that all the ingredients are just covered (about 4 cups), no more. Bring to a boil for a few minutes, then reduce the heat, cover, and simmer, stirring occasionally, until the potatoes are cooked through, about 30 minutes.

3. Once the potatoes are cooked, give them a little beating up with a spoon. Add more salt, pepper, tamari, or Worcestershire if needed. Turn off the heat and cover to keep the stovies warm until you are ready to eat.

THOM FILICIA

Interior designer

Unfortunately, I eat everything—literally, everything. I enjoy food from high to low, from cooked to uncooked, unusual to extraordinarily typical. People ask, "Why do you think that is?" And I say, my mom used to make food fun.

My mother was Italian. She was a great cook, and she loved entertaining. So my life growing up was always centered around dinner parties and lots of food, lots of joy, and lots of booze. I think her love was first and foremost of food and the sharing of stories and telling stories; she was very theatrical. My mother would always say, tell a dirty joke and you'll quickly figure out who's up for a good time and who's not.

She always prepared delicious meals and served them really beautifully. I can't tell you how many times I had to clean the silver or help set tables or take coats and keep them organized. I had tons of jobs like that. Delivering cocktails, too. I poured a lot of Scotch for a kid under 12.

When I was really little, instead of going to bed I used to hide under the dining table during her parties. It was an old house and it had a bell in the floor that rang in the kitchen. When I fell asleep on it they would hear it ringing and know that I'd been eavesdropping. I always got busted by the bell.

The dish I miss most is my mother's famous Thanksgiving oyster stuffing. She got the oysters from a local place the day of, and she always made her own bread crumbs—she was very specific about everything. Then she would cook the stuffing inside the bird. As a kid I wasn't a huge fan of turkey so for me it was all about the oyster stuffing, which sounds bizarre, but I loved it. I know it seems like a side, but the way that my mother made it, it was totally a main dish. Or at least I thought it was. And I love what it does to the turkey. It gives the meat a really nice flavor and makes everything a little bit more wonderful. My least favorite word on the planet is "moist" but I think her stuffing was more moist than it was supposed to be on purpose, and that's what made it so amazing. It's like when you under-bake cookies.

Thanksgiving was always a classic family event. It was always boisterous. And it was always really great food. More than anything, the next-day leftovers—and, as I got older, Bloody Marys—were the most coveted part of the holiday experience. My mother prided herself on making fabulous Bloody Marys. She used to make them with Clamato juice, but then as I got older, she started using V8 because she thought it was healthier.

So food for me is not just about the pleasure of eating and the expression of love through cooking, but also the festivity of the meal, as well as the conversation and the humor that's shared—it's a celebration of life. That's how I grew up. A lot of things happened around the dining room table.

Janet's "Land & Sea" Oyster Stuffing

Serves 8 to 12

4 tablespoons unsalted butter, more for greasing the pan

2 stalks celery, diced

1 cup diced onion

4 scallions, white and green parts, thinly sliced

Pinch of cayenne

3 cups dry stuffing cubes

3 cups dry Italian bread crumbs

½ cup minced fresh flat-leaf parsley, more for garnish

Kosher salt and freshly ground black pepper

2 large eggs, lightly beaten

1 pint shucked fresh oysters and their liquid (you will need ½ cup liquid; use clam juice to supplement if you don't have enough)

1. Preheat the oven to 350°F. Lightly butter a 9 by 13-inch baking pan.

2. Melt half of the butter in a skillet over medium-low heat. Add the celery, onion, and scallions and cook, stirring, until softened. Remove from heat, stir in the cayenne, and let cool slightly.

3. Combine the stuffing cubes and bread crumbs in a large bowl. Gently fold in the sautéed vegetables and parsley; season with salt and pepper. Add the beaten eggs and toss to distribute. Strain the oysters over a bowl and add the oyster liquid (and/or clam juice) to the stuffing. The mixture should be moist but not soggy. Gently fold in the oysters. Dot the top with the remaining 2 tablespoons of butter.

4. Cover the stuffing with foil and bake 30 minutes. Remove the foil and continue baking until the top is golden brown, about another 30 minutes. Serve.

SUVIR SARAN
Chef, author, public speaker, hobby farmer

Panditji, our family's chef, used to make this dish for my mother's very fancy parties when I was a child. I loved those parties: the table was lavishly set with our best china, silverware, and linens, and we all feasted on a vast array of exquisite foods complemented by Panditji's best pickles and other delicacies.

Appetizers of several types would keep the guests busy as we waited for everyone to arrive. We use the term IST to mean "Indian stretchable time," as we Indians are famous for always being late. Seasonal drinks, fruits, and music all found their way into the festivities. Flowers were always used to add brilliance and scent.

Three or four generations of relatives and close friends would show up at these gatherings. I would look to these lunches in the winter and dinners in the summer as a way to soak in the brilliance of Indian textiles. All the women would be adorned in beautiful jewels and saris, contrasting blouses, matching earrings, necklaces, bracelets, and clutches. As a gay man, this was my inspiration, just as much as the food that Panditji would cook.

Meals would always include much laughter and light, nonmalicious gossiping and teasing among the grown-ups and kids. Children in India are never kept away from adults. Politics, religion, jokes (politically incorrect ones too) are all part of our upbringing. We learn early on about life and its challenges. There were often rigorous debates, even tense arguments—but nothing good food and family couldn't keep civilized and in perspective.

Invariably my grandmother, or my beloved father, would end up asking me to perform a song, which would become several songs, and then another kid—or adult or my grandaunts or granduncles—would sing. It often led to dancing…

Being a Brahman chef, Panditji was not a fan of visitors coming into his kitchen, which was also the home to his little temple-cabinet, filled with idols of the many gods and goddesses of India. And so it was important to him that

people enter his domain freshly showered, without leather and footwear, and with respect for the space and the mini altar it contained. I, however, was given free reign, and I loved being there. This was my hiding spot. A place where I sought comfort and, from a young age, felt I belonged. In the kitchen with Panditji, I found peace, creativity, and a total absence of judgment. Most of all, I found in Panditji a kind older man, who was there for me and indulged me, no matter what I did.

My fondest memories are of those times spent watching Panditji mix spices and chop the same vegetable in many different ways toward different end results. I saw him cook and create, share and delight—not out of ego, but out of a deep dedication to his work, to our family, and to pleasing others with his food.

I make this dish now for special occasions because it never fails to impress. Often I serve the cauliflower sitting atop cumin-scented green peas, which add a luscious contrast to the red of the sauce. I think of this as a vegetarian roast: a wonderfully delicious bite that is equally at ease as a main course as it is as a side.

For this Mogul dish, a whole head of cauliflower is first steamed until almost tender (Panditji taught me to add a little milk to the water to keep the cauliflower white), then deep-fried to enhance its flavor, and finally glazed with a spiced tomato sauce. Because it takes some time to make and reheats well, I always prepare it in advance and warm it up in the oven just before serving.

Party Cauliflower with Indian-Spiced Tomato Sauce

Serves 6

2 large red onions, coarsely chopped

1½-inch piece fresh ginger, peeled and sliced

2 medium cloves garlic, peeled

1 teaspoon kosher salt, more for seasoning

1 (28-ounce) can whole tomatoes in puree, including puree

½ teaspoon garam masala

3 tablespoons vegetable oil, plus 6 to 10 cups for frying

1-inch cinnamon stick

5 whole cloves

3 bay leaves

1 tablespoon ground coriander

½ teaspoon ground cumin

¼ teaspoon ground turmeric

¼ teaspoon cayenne

1 large head cauliflower, leaves cut off and stem trimmed flat

2 tablespoons milk

1. To make the tomato sauce, put the onion, ginger, garlic, and 1 teaspoon of salt in a food processor and process to a paste. Transfer to a small bowl and set aside. Add the tomatoes in puree and the garam masala to the processor and puree until smooth. Set aside.

2. Put 3 tablespoons of vegetable oil, cinnamon, cloves, and bay leaves in a wide, heavy 5-quart pot. Cook over medium-high heat, stirring, until the cinnamon unfurls, 1 to 2 minutes. Add the onion paste and cook, stirring frequently, until the onion starts to brown around the edges, about 10 minutes. Add the coriander, cumin, turmeric, and cayenne and cook, stirring, 1 minute. Add 2 tablespoons water and cook, stirring, until the onion begins to stick to the pan, about 1 minute more. Add the tomato puree and cook, stirring frequently, 5 minutes. Add more salt if needed. Keep warm.

3. To prepare the cauliflower, bring an inch of water and the milk to a boil in a wide pot large enough to hold the whole head. Put the cauliflower in the pot, stem side down. Cover the pot and steam the cauliflower until just beginning to soften—pierce with a paring knife to test—4 to 5 minutes. Transfer using two slotted spoons to a plate and discard the water.

4. Fill a wok (or the cleaned and dried pot) with 1½ to 2 inches of oil and heat over medium-high heat to 375°F. Carefully lower the cauliflower, top side down, into the oil with 2 slotted spoons. It should cover the head halfway. Fry until golden brown, 1 to 2 minutes. Using the slotted spoons, carefully turn it over and brown the underside, 2 to 3 minutes. Transfer the cauliflower to paper towels to drain.

5. Put the cauliflower on a serving dish (or baking dish if planning to reheat later on) and pour enough sauce over it to cover completely; if you've made it ahead of time, reheat in a 300°F oven for about 15 minutes. Cut it into wedges and serve.

Editor's note: *You will have more tomato sauce than you need for the dish, but it is so delicious, you'll want to try it on everything!*

PHILIP GALANES

Journalist, lawyer

Let's call this story "Two Closets and a Snack."

On a thick summer's day, when I was 14 years old, my mother took it into her head to inspect the cedar closet. (I know! Who sorts woolens in the heat of August?) Being a thorough woman, she quickly discovered the *Playgirl* magazine I had shoplifted from our neighborhood grocer and stashed in the folds of an old plaid blanket. I consulted that magazine frequently, hoping each time that I would no longer thrill to the dark-haired centerfold with his sly grin—

but I never grew tired of him.

I didn't know about my mother's cedar closet doings that day. When I next saw her—carrying my smutty magazine in one hand and a red Shetland sweater in the other—I was sitting in another closet, the one she shared with my father, trying to shove my foot into a high-heeled shoe with a satin bow at the back.

"I never liked those," my mother said.

I knew enough to keep quiet.

I don't remember much more, but I can call up my shame and my mother's rough kindness as if it were this morning. I begged her not to tell my father; she hugged me hard when I started to cry. And soon after, she began ferrying me to a child psychiatrist whose office was in a regular house like ours. After the sessions, she drove me home, and we shared a favorite snack: Lebanese za'atar bread that her mother had taught her to bake.

Za'atar Flatbreads

Makes 8 flatbreads

1 cup warm water

1 teaspoon active dry yeast

1 teaspoon granulated sugar

3 cups all-purpose flour

1 teaspoon kosher salt

½ cup olive oil, more for oiling the dough and baking sheets

6 tablespoons za'atar*

*Za'atar is a mixture of sesame seeds, powdered sumac berries, and dried wild thyme. It can be found in Middle Eastern markets or online at Kalustyans.com.

1. Put ¼ cup of the warm water in a small bowl and add yeast and sugar. Let stand 10 minutes, until creamy.

2. Put the flour and salt in a large bowl and stir with your fingers to combine. Add the yeast mixture and stir in the remaining ¾ cup warm water. (If the dough is too dry, add water; if too wet, add flour.) Transfer the dough to a work surface and knead with your hands until smooth and elastic, about 10 minutes.

3. Form dough into a ball, oil lightly, put in a large bowl, cover with a cloth or plastic wrap, and let stand until doubled in size, about 1 hour.

4. Divide the dough into 8 portions and form each into a small ball.

5. Lightly oil 2 large rimmed baking sheets. On each sheet, using your fingers press 4 balls into circles of 5 to 6 inches in diameter and ¼ inch thick. Make some small depressions in the surface of the circles with your fingertips.

6. Preheat the oven to 400°F.

7. Combine the ½ cup olive oil and za'atar in a small bowl, then divide the mixture among the breads, spreading with the back of a spoon.

8. Bake the breads, one sheet at a time, until bottoms are browned, about 8 to 10 minutes.

9. Preheat the broiler. Broil the breads until the tops are lightly browned, 1 to 2 minutes. Serve warm.

BILL T. JONES

Director, choreographer

It was the fall of 1992 and I was visiting Paris as the guest of my new friend, Bjorn Amelan. I arrived at his apartment at dinnertime. My first impression was one of surprise at the elegance and whimsy of the apartment's decoration, wherein important works by French designer Jean Royère provided a sort of stage set for numerous objects of black memorabilia—such as mammy dolls, golliwogs, and Jazz Age posters—curious and colorful bric-a-brac that spoke to another era, a festive reminder of

a sober fact: these were the artifacts of the partnership Bjorn had shared with talented African-American fashion designer Patrick Kelly, who had died two years prior.

Just as surprising was the menu: fried chicken, corn bread, and candied yams. Many thousands of miles away from my ancestral roots in the Deep South and years away from my mother's cooking, feeling a bit like a wayfaring stranger in a foreign country, unable to speak the language and embarking on a new friendship, I found great comfort in this menu as it illuminated how past, present, and future could coalesce in a moment, in a meal. This dinner presaged the partnership we were about to embark on and which now, 22 years later, we still share.

Corn Bread

Serves 9

½ cup yellow cornmeal

½ cup all-purpose flour

1 tablespoon baking powder

½ teaspoon fine salt

¾ cup full-fat plain yogurt

1 large egg

¼ cup vegetable oil

1. Preheat the oven to 425°F.

2. Stir the dry ingredients together in a bowl. Whisk together the yogurt, egg, oil, and ¼ cup of water in a small bowl and stir into the flour mixture.

3. Pour the batter into a 9-inch cast-iron skillet and bake until a toothpick comes out clean, about 20 minutes. Serve warm.

PASTA
&
GRAINS

MARK BITTMAN
Food journalist, cookbook author

My mother didn't cook elaborate feasts, but she cooked every night. By today's standards, that may be even more impressive, though at the time it was neither revolutionary nor romantic. The shopping and cooking that go into even the simplest meals were all a part of the daily routine, and I didn't take much interest in them.

When I started to cook in college, it was out of necessity and not interest—the cafeteria food drove me to find something better. Eventually—not long afterward—it became, essentially, a passion, so much so that when I started writing for a living, the natural subject was cooking. The more I did of one thing, the more I learned about the other.

Most of my cooking happened—and still happens—alone in my kitchen, where I, like my mother, made dinner every night for myself and my family. (My kids are now women.) But it's equally valuable and intriguing to see how someone else does the job, so I've spent a lot of time in other people's kitchens. I've cooked with world-renowned chefs and I've cooked with people who've hardly picked up a knife. You never cook with someone without learning something.

My favorite people to learn from are "grandmother cooks," people who carry forth food traditions that might otherwise die. When Marcella Hazan came to America from Cesenatico, Italy, there wasn't much more to Italian-American food than red sauce. Her cookbooks introduced leagues of home cooks to simple Italian cuisine and got many of us thinking about the importance of cooking with fresh, good ingredients. Her recipes, universally, are accessible and

without pretense. In following them, not only do you put meals on the table, but you also learn about what it really means to cook normal food.

This pasta is one that I learned from Marcella decades ago and have made about ten times a year ever since. Sometimes I swap the cauliflower for another vegetable, or maybe I'll add chopped anchovies or tomatoes. It continues to evolve in my kitchen, as I hope it will in yours.

Pasta with Cauliflower

Serves 4

Kosher salt

1 head cauliflower, about 1 pound

½ cup extra-virgin olive oil

1 cup coarse bread crumbs, preferably homemade

1 pound penne, fusilli, or other cut pasta

1 tablespoon minced fresh garlic

Freshly ground black pepper

1. Fill a large pot with water and about a tablespoon of salt and bring to a boil.

2. Trim the cauliflower and cut it into large florets, then add to the pot and boil until they are quite tender but not mushy, 5 to 8 minutes. Using a slotted spoon or strainer, remove the cauliflower florets and set aside. Leave the water in the pot and let it come back up to a boil.

3. Meanwhile, heat ¼ cup of the oil in a large, deep skillet over medium heat, then add the bread crumbs and cook, stirring, until crisp and golden, about 5 minutes. Transfer to paper towels to drain.

4. Chop the cauliflower into small pieces. Add the pasta to the pot and cook until 2 or 3 minutes short of the way you like it. Drain, reserving about a cup of the cooking liquid.

5. While the pasta is cooking, heat the remaining ¼ cup of oil in the skillet over medium-low heat, add the garlic, and cook, stirring, until the garlic begins to turn golden. Add the cauliflower, increase the heat to medium, and cook, stirring, until golden, about 5 minutes.

6. Add the pasta to the skillet and toss everything with a large spoon until it's well combined. Add salt and pepper; stir in just enough pasta water to keep the mixture moist but not soupy, and cook until the pasta is the way you like it. Mix in the bread crumbs and serve.

APRIL GORNIK & ERIC FISCHL
Artists

We are both crazy about Italy—Rome in particular—and who doesn't love Italian food? In fact, we got married in Rome in 1998, which involved climbing a small mountain of paperwork and apologies, from both the Italian Consulate and State Department simultaneously, about how the other was making the whole process unnecessarily complicated. But it was all worth it!

We spent five weeks at the American Academy in Rome in 2006, and took the opportunity to hire a tutor to help us learn a little proper Italian. Rosa was an older lady, who animatedly and patiently described to us the difference between the various names, for instance, for sacks of foodstuffs for al-

most anything you could buy at a market (beans have their own sacks, flour its own, etc.). She worked hard and came to us around 1pm. After a couple of classes, we thought she was looking exhausted and so we decided to offer her lunch. I love to make pasta, and I also love to invent pasta dishes, so I'd go to the market, order the right things in the wrong bags, and then innocently put ingredients together in—what seemed to her—outrageous combinations. I don't think we ever served her a pasta she didn't look horrified at, but then after she had explained why, for instance, an Italian would *never* combine radicchio and pleurottes (oyster mushrooms) served with *that* kind of cheese, she invariably had seconds, which gave us great pleasure.

Spaghetti Aglio-Olio with Fresh Herbs

Serves 2

2 tablespoons kosher salt

8 ounces dried spaghetti

3 tablespoons extra-virgin olive oil

2 large cloves garlic, thinly sliced

6 sun-dried tomatoes, finely chopped (⅓ cup)

½ teaspoon finely chopped fresh rosemary

¾ ounce finely grated aged pecorino (¾ cup using a rasp grater)

2 tablespoons finely sliced fresh basil

¼ cup finely chopped fresh chives

¼ cup finely chopped fresh parsley

1. Bring a large pot of water to a boil and add the kosher salt. Add the spaghetti and cook according to package directions until al dente.

2. While the pasta is cooking, heat the oil and the garlic in a large skillet over medium heat, stirring until the garlic is pale golden, about 5 minutes. Add the dried tomatoes and rosemary and cook, stirring, 1 minute. (Set aside if the spaghetti isn't ready.)

3. Drain the spaghetti, reserving 1 cup of the cooking water.

4. Add ½ cup of the cooking water and ¼ cup of the cheese to the skillet. Add the spaghetti and toss to combine, adding more pasta cooking water if necessary.

5. Transfer to a large heated bowl, add the basil, chives, and parsley, and toss to combine. Serve with the remaining cheese.

LINDA FAIRSTEIN

Crime novelist

I spent a lot of time in the kitchen as a child, watching the two women I adored most—my mother and my maternal grandmother—lovingly and creatively prepare meals for our family. They both took enormous pleasure in cooking, so sitting at the dinner table was an hour filled with storytelling and recounting the day's events—whether tales from the hospital operating room in which my father worked, or my mother's volunteer duties as an RN, or my brother and my adventures at school.

I wanted to learn to cook, to enjoy what my mother and grandmother found so satisfying in nourishing their family. But it made no sense to me. Hours of shopping to find the freshest produce and best fish or meat, then more long hours at the sink and stove, then a relatively swift devouring of the good food by everyone at the table before moving on to the unsavory process of washing dishes. So I abandoned that interest in cooking early in life, but I cling to the memories of the joy those meals occasioned.

When I began to transition from my prosecutorial career to my life as an author, I spent more and more time on Martha's Vineyard, most happily with family around me. To the very end of her long, well-lived life, my mother still delighted in cooking for everyone, and my favorite recipe is one she made frequently when the tiny, sweet Nantucket Bay scallops were available at her favorite fish market in the village of Menemsha.

Bobbie's Angel-Hair Pasta with Scallops and Shallots

Serves 4

1 pound bay scallops, tough muscles removed

¼ cup extra-virgin olive oil

½ cup chopped shallots

¾ pound angel-hair pasta

3 tablespoons chopped fresh flat-leaf parsley

2 tablespoons fresh lemon juice

½ teaspoon freshly ground black pepper

1 teaspoon kosher salt

Finely grated lemon zest for garnish

The dish tastes best with some heated garlic bread to sop up the sauce, and a delicious bottle of chilled white wine.

1. Bring a large pot of salted water to a boil. Pat the scallops dry and have all your ingredients ready.

2. Heat the olive oil in a 12-inch skillet over medium heat. Add the shallots to the skillet and cook, stirring, until they begin to color, about 3 minutes.

3. Add the pasta to the boiling water and cook according to package directions until al dente, 2 to 3 minutes.

4. While the pasta is cooking, add the scallops to the skillet and cook, stirring, until they become opaque, 2 to 3 minutes, and remove from the heat. (You have to keep a close watch on them! Scallops cook quickly and become way too chewy if overdone.) Add the parsley, lemon juice, pepper, and salt to the scallops and stir.

5. Drain the pasta, reserving 1 cup of the cooking water. Add the pasta to the scallops and toss to combine, adding enough of the reserved pasta cooking water to moisten. Sprinkle a little grated lemon zest on top and serve immediately.

JON ROBIN BAITZ

Playwright, screenwriter

This dish (in its original form) was a sort of 1980s LA bit of fabulousness. Supposedly invented late one night at Le Dome, a movie/music-biz hangout on Sunset Strip, it is quintessentially Californian in that it is incredibly simple, vaguely glamorous, and makes you feel good. I used to have it there occasionally, but I think I might have improved on it a little bit. Le Dome is gone, as is most of the old '30s-to-'70s movie culture that made LA so very cool for so long.

But that's another story. It's a very good dish for date night, because caviar shared with too many people seems a little too last-days-of-Rome for me. I made it the first time my boyfriend came to dinner, and we're still together—we're married now—and Leon saved the empty caviar jar as a memento. (I cleaned it first.)

This meal should not take more than 20 minutes to make. I recommend using really good butter (but not salted, please, or it's just a disaster and your taste buds go into shock and the meal is ruined and your life is made less joyous and your date person will never ever return and you will end up all alone forever because you used butter with salt). Cook the spaghetti till it's al dente. But not too al dente. Frank Sinatra once fired his valet (and threw the pasta at him) for serving his spaghetti too al dente. And if you like, there is nothing to prevent you from adding some boiled new potatoes—little ones—sliced into sort of dime-sized pieces. I have done this to good effect.

Serve with a nice glass of Pinot Gris from Willamette Valley in Oregon, and play something on the turntable, but nothing too twee, for God's sake. It should be dichotomous to the dish, so Stephen Malkmus or the Pixies' "Here Comes Your Man." Or maybe Silver Jews. But not Bacharach. It will ruin the pasta. I love Bacharach but too much Pacific Coast Highway lassitude will do you in. And there will be no sex that night or any other.

At dinner discuss e.e. cummings, Ennio Morricone, the Knicks, and Jean Pierre Melville movies. No mention of musicals. Or deconstructionists, or post-

Marxist theory. Do not add opera to the conversation or cats (neither the musical or the creatures). Ed Ruscha, Marfa Texas, and mangos from India are good topics. Nobody cares to discuss the horrors of the GOP on date night. Really. No. If you want to talk about a great book, read the late Evan S. Connell's *Son of the Morning Star: General Custer and the Battle of the Little Bighorn*—but only in the original Northpoint Press edition, hardback. And, also pre-date, read *City of Nets*, by Otto Freidrich, about German intellectuals who fled to Hollywood before and during World War II. A truly magisterial book about Hollywood culture.

I think one should have sex at the end of this evening. Safely, but passionately. Some people think sex is over, but I think it's just begun.

Date-Night Spaghetti with Vodka and Caviar

Serves 2, with leftovers

2 tablespoons kosher salt

1 pound spaghetti

2 tablespoons unsalted butter

2 medium shallots, chopped

½ cup vodka (Tito's is a good choice)

2 to 3 tablespoons fresh lemon juice

½ cup heavy cream

2 ounces American sturgeon caviar or salmon roe

Maldon salt and freshly ground black pepper

1. Bring a large pot of water to a boil and add the kosher salt. Cook the pasta until al dente and drain, reserving 1 cup of pasta water.

2. When the pasta is almost ready, melt the butter in a large skillet over medium-low heat, add the shallots and cook, stirring, until translucent. Add the vodka and 2 tablespoons of lemon juice and cook 1 minute. Add the cream, bring to a simmer, and season with the Maldon salt, black pepper, and more lemon juice if desired.

3. Add the drained pasta to the sauce and toss to coat. Add a little of the reserved pasta water if it seems dry. Divide between plates and top with the caviar.

ALEXANDRA WENTWORTH & GEORGE STEPHANOPOULOS

Author, actor / Television news anchor

I like to think that my winning personality and passable looks resulted in true love. But I sometimes think that the pasta with sausage Bolognese may have been the special sauce in my love story.

When I met my husband, George, it was love at first sight, first speak, and first smell. We were set up on a blind date, which resulted in lunch and a mutual admiration of crab salad. We parted ways that day smitten and with a handshake.

Our next date took place at George's apartment—a real bachelor pad with a sparse kitchen and an unplugged refrigerator used for storing files and magazine articles. There was one pot, a couple spoons, and a few salt packets from an antiquated take-out order. Instead of heading out to the newest Pan-Asian restaurant, I decided to make dinner!

I settled on a recipe that I have tinkered with over the years, but originally tasted at the River Café in Brooklyn: the infamous penne with sausage sauce. A recipe with enough heartiness, zest, and spice to ensure a fabulous and romantic feast.

We dined outside on his miniscule deck with a couple candles stuck in bottles and a gigantic bowl of the dishy dish.

We were engaged two months later…

Even after 13 years together, when I make this dish for our children and friends, George always proclaims, "This is the dish Ali made me on our second date!"

It should be renamed "pasta with happily-ever-after sauce"!

Pasta with Spicy Sausage Bolognese

Serves 2 (with enough leftover sauce for another meal)

2 tablespoons olive oil

2 small red onions, chopped

5 spicy Italian sausages, casings removed and meat crumbled

1½ tablespoons chopped fresh rosemary

2 bay leaves

2 small dried chilies, crumbled, optional

9 ounces penne rigate

1 (28-ounce) can peeled plum tomatoes in juice, drained and chopped

⅔ cup heavy cream

4 ounces Parmigiano-Reggiano, freshly grated

Sea salt and freshly ground black pepper

1. In a wide 4- to 5-quart heavy pot, heat the oil over medium heat and cook the onions until lightly browned. Add the crumbled sausage, the rosemary, bay leaves, and chilies, if desired. Cook over medium-high heat, stirring and breaking up the sausage meat until it has rendered its fat.

2. Remove all but 1 tablespoon of the fat from the pot, and continue to cook, stirring occasionally, until the meat is browned and disintegrated, about 20 minutes.

3. Meanwhile, cook the penne in a pot of boiling salted water according to package directions, then drain thoroughly and return to the pot.

4. Stir the tomatoes into the pot with the sausage and bring to a boil. Stir in the cream and half of the grated cheese and return to a boil. Season with salt and pepper if needed.

5. Spoon half of the sauce over the pasta on two plates, or mix the sauce together with the pasta (reserve the remaining sauce for another meal). Serve the remaining grated cheese on the side.

MIKE LUPICA
Author

We have always called it "Ohio Girl" lasagna in our family.
It is prepared by my wife, Taylor, with skill and care and love, and if you ask our four children what their favorite dish is, the vote would be unanimous. Mom's lasagna, they would tell you, prepared by the former Taylor McKelvy, out of Perrysburg, Ohio—her own recipe, better than any lasagna I have ever had in an Italian restaurant anywhere.

"Even the slop," they would also tell you, meaning the parts of it that become soupy every time they are too impatient to allow their mother to let the food cool as long as she wants it to.

But it is not just this Italian dish prepared by the Ohio Girl, as delicious as it always is, that makes it such a special event at our dining-room table and in our family and in our home. No. What makes it special is the conversation that comes along with it, like some wonderful side dish, and the laughter; how it reminds our children and shows their friends all the love around that table, in our family, in our home.

There are so many other things, hundreds of them, big and small, that bind and hold a family together. There are stories and shared history and memory. But the dinner table is so often at the center of it all, me at one end and Taylor at the other, two of our boys to her right, and usually our youngest son and daughter to her left. And a friend or two, or three, sharing in the food, and the conversation, and the laughter, before they head back into the kitchen for seconds.

Or thirds.

We sit down at that long old table for Ohio Girl lasagna and suddenly it is not just that night, it is all the nights. I see our amazing children as they are, but also as they were, as if the only unchanging thing in the room is the food in front of us.

I see college boys going up for seconds now, when the college boys are home, and I see them as high-school boys. And junior-high-school boys before that.

My youngest son's best friend in high school was a boy named Kevin Mahoney. He would go to the kitchen for seconds and if there was any hesitation, it meant that there wasn't much lasagna left; we had all cleaned out Taylor again.

And she knew. She has always known.

"Finish it, Kevin," she'd call into the kitchen, and he would, happily.

You would love the food, I promise you. And you'd be one of those going for seconds. Even for the slop. Or especially for the slop. But you would love being at that table more.

Classic Lasagna with Sausage

Serves 8

12 lasagna noodles (from a 1-pound box)

1 pound sweet Italian sausages, casings removed

1½ (24-ounce) jars Rao's marinara sauce

Kosher salt and freshly ground black pepper

3 (8-ounce) containers small-curd 4 percent cottage cheese

2 (8-ounce) bags grated whole-milk mozzarella cheese

1. Bring a large pot of salted water to a boil over high heat. Boil the lasagna noodles in batches according to package directions. Carefully remove the noodles as they finish cooking and lay them on clean cloth towels (not terry cloth) in one layer.

2. Crumble the sausage into a large skillet and cook over medium heat, stirring, until browned and cooked through, about 5 minutes. Drain off any excess fat. Add the marinara sauce and simmer with sausage for a few minutes. Season with salt and pepper if needed.

3. Preheat the oven to 400°F.

4. In a 9 by 13-inch baking dish, spread a small amount of the sauce to sparsely cover the bottom. Arrange 4 noodles on top, spread with about a third of the sauce, dab with a third of the cottage cheese, and sprinkle with a third of the mozzarella. Repeat 2 more times, starting with the noodles and ending with the mozzarella.

5. Bake until bubbling and browned on top, 50 minutes to 1 hour. Let stand 10 to 15 minutes before serving.

LANCE BASS

Host, singer, producer

My grandmother Mimi and I have a very special relationship. We lived next door to her until I was about eight years old and we saw each other every day. I'd go over to her house and she'd always be in the kitchen making something delicious. Mimi's the cook in the family and definitely one of my biggest inspirations in the kitchen. What I love about her Chicken Ro-tel in particular, is that for as long as I can remember, it's been a staple in all of our holiday meals.

The holidays are really just an excuse for us Southerners to get together and eat. Easter, Halloween, Groundhog Day, you name it, in the South we'll celebrate anything! Whenever I'm with my family, everything always revolves around food and this particular dish has been a big part of that. Mimi passed the recipe on to my mom, who now cooks it at every holiday meal—and often in between—and it has become the one thing I love to make and what my friends request most when we have get-togethers or go to a potluck. When I take a bite of Chicken Ro-tel, it brings me back to every single Thanksgiving I've ever had, because I can just taste what that day tasted like. It reminds me of my Mimi and it describes Mississippi to a T, because we love our casseroles, plus it's hard to go wrong with loads of cheese!

Because of that, it's definitely a recipe you can only eat every once in a while—but that's what's so special about the holidays. You forget about that diet for one day and you get to just indulge—and there's no denying, this dish is definitely an indulgence! Now when I make it, I only put in one package of Velveeta instead of two, but Mimi says that as long as it's made with love, it's all good.

Chicken Ro*Tel

Serves 10 to 12

1 teaspoon kosher salt, more for boiling pasta

1 pound spaghetti

4 ounces (1 stick) unsalted butter, more to grease the casserole dish

1 green bell pepper, chopped

1 onion, chopped

1 rotisserie chicken, bones removed, meat coarsely chopped

1 pound Velveeta or cheddar cheese, grated

1 (10-ounce) can Ro*Tel tomatoes and green chilies

1 (10.5-ounce) can cream of mushroom soup

1 tablespoon Worcestershire sauce

½ teaspoon freshly ground black pepper

1. Preheat the oven to 350°F.

2. Meanwhile, bring a large pot of salted water to a boil and cook the spaghetti according to package directions. Drain and transfer to a large bowl.

3. Melt the butter in a skillet over medium heat and cook the pepper and onion, stirring, until the onion is soft but not colored, about 10 minutes. Add to the spaghetti in the bowl, along with the chicken, cheese, tomatoes, soup, Worcestershire sauce, salt, and pepper.

4. Transfer the mixture to a 4-quart buttered casserole and bake until hot and bubbly, about 45 minutes. Put under the broiler for several minutes to brown, if desired. Let stand a few minutes before serving.

CYNDI LAUPER

Artist, activist

Many years ago, a director I worked with named Ed Bianci gave me his family recipe for risotto. It was one of the best I'd ever tasted. He'd learned it from his mom and he taught it to (lucky) me.

I love making this dish because it's really just an excuse for a fun gathering of friends. You can sit around the kitchen together, talking, drinking wine, taking turns stirring the rice—you pour some wine in the risotto, then you pour a

little wine for your friends. So choose a wine to cook with that you also want to drink. I like an Italian wine, particularly Pinot Grigio, when I eat or prepare Italian food. But that's me. I'm Italian.

Get a bunch of asparagus. Now everyone always says size matters, and that's exactly how I feel about the asparagus. Except I like the asparagus thin. It's not so tough. Also you want Italian rice— Aborio or Carnaroli. You'll need a medium onion, six cups of chicken stock (if you're a vegetarian, then get vegetable stock), and white wine. You'll also need a stick of butter, and a pinch of saffron.

Take your onion and finely dice it. Also wash and cut up the asparagus into one-inch pieces. But don't use the bottom of the asparagus. I like to cut off an inch and a half of the bottom. The top is more tender. Put the asparagus aside.

Then take half a stick of butter—my friend Ed's family, they used a whole stick of butter, but me, I was worried it was too much like a heart attack waiting to happen, so I changed it to half a stick of butter. Anyway, it's up to you. In a deep, medium-sized frying pan, melt the butter and then sauté the onion till it caramelizes. You'll need to use a low flame. It has to cook slowly, that's how it

gets creamy. When the chopped onion is caramelized, it'll be translucent. Add one cup of the uncooked rice and stir. Then add one cup of white wine and stir until the liquid cooks away. After that, add a cup of stock and stir until the liquid cooks away. Continue until you've gone through five cups of stock. On the sixth cup you should add the chopped asparagus and stir until it reduces. Then add the saffron for color.

Get a nice-size bowl and put the risotto in it and serve.

Buono appetito, baby!

Ed's Asparagus Risotto

Serves 4

2 ounces (½ stick) salted butter

1 medium onion, finely
    chopped (1¼ cups)

1 cup raw Arborio or
    Carnaroli rice

1 cup dry white wine,
    preferably Pinot Grigio

6 cups chicken stock or
    vegetable stock

1 pound fresh thin asparagus,
    tough ends trimmed; cut into
    1-inch pieces

2 strands of saffron

1. Melt the butter in a wide 4-quart pot over medium heat. Add onion, turn the heat to low, and cook, stirring occasionally, until the onion is translucent. You'll need to stay there and watch.

2. When the onions are ready, increase the heat to medium, add the rice, and cook, stirring, 1 minute.

3. Add the wine and cook over medium heat, stirring, until it is absorbed. You need to stay there stirring.

4. Keep the heat on medium and start adding stock 1 cup at a time, stirring constantly until the liquid is mostly absorbed, then add the next cup and do the same.

5. When you finally get to the 6th cup of stock, add the asparagus and continue stirring until the rice is tender but not too mushy and the asparagus are just tender. The risotto should be creamy. Taste it and see what consistency you like, and also how tender or al dente you like.

6. Here is where you add 2 strands of saffron for color.

Cyndi's note: *If you sit and stir the whole time (and, again, you should taste a little too so you know what you are cooking tastes like), the risotto will come out pretty great.*

EMMY ROSSUM

Actor

I grew up in a small apartment in New York City with a single mom. From as early as I can remember, it was always just the two of us. The tiny kitchen was our favorite place and it was about more than just making food. It was about love and learning. It was where my mom would halve or double recipes to help me with math. It was where I would sing silly made-up songs at the top of my lungs and where I would eventually learn to deglaze a pan and make a crème brûlée. I can still remember the aromas of melting cheese and sautéed vegetables filling our little apartment on cold winter nights after I'd get home from school.

My mom used to make a delicious variation of this ratatouille recipe all the time when I was a kid. It's a pretty inexpensive dish to make, and it's nutritious. Nowadays, I like to cook it during the winter on Sunday evenings with friends or on "meatless Mondays."

Fried Polenta with Sautéed Vegetables

Serves 4 to 6 as a first course

¼ cup milk, more to thin

1 cup instant polenta, more for sprinkling on polenta cakes

4 tablespoons unsalted butter

2 tablespoons freshly grated Parmesan cheese

Kosher salt and freshly ground black pepper

4 teaspoons red wine vinegar

½ teaspoon Dijon mustard

3 tablespoons extra-virgin olive oil

1 each small (4-ounce) red, green, and yellow bell peppers, halved and seeded

1. In a 2-quart saucepan, bring the milk to a boil over medium heat. Whisk in the polenta, lower the heat, and simmer, stirring occasionally, until smooth, 3 to 5 minutes. Add extra milk if the mixture is too thick. Stir in 2 tablespoons of the butter and Parmesan and season with salt and pepper. Transfer the polenta to a greased baking sheet and spread it out to a 6-inch square about ½ inch thick. Let cool, then refrigerate until set, at least 1 hour.

2. In a small bowl, whisk together the vinegar, mustard, a pinch of salt, and a pinch of ground black pepper. Slowly whisk in the olive oil, adjust the seasoning, and set the vinaigrette aside.

3. Preheat the broiler on high.

4. Put the peppers, skin side up, on a baking sheet and broil until blackened. Transfer the peppers to a sealable plastic bag and seal to steam them for 5 minutes. Remove the skins and dice the peppers.

2 tablespoons olive oil

1 small zucchini, diced

1 small eggplant, diced

⅔ cup sun-dried tomatoes, diced

4 cloves garlic, minced

2 tablespoons chopped tomatoes

Mint leaves, for garnish

5. Heat the oil in a skillet over medium heat. Add the peppers, zucchini, eggplant, sun-dried tomatoes, and garlic and cook, stirring, until tender, about 10 minutes. Stir in the tomatoes and the vinaigrette, remove from heat, and season with salt and pepper.

6. Cut the polenta into 4 squares, trangles, or diamonds. Sprinkle with a little dry polenta on both sides. Heat the remaining 2 tablespoons of butter in a large skillet over medium heat until the foam from the butter subsides and add the polenta cakes. Fry until golden brown on both sides, 6 to 10 minutes total, and transfer to salad plates. Top each polenta cake with the vegetables and garnish with mint leaves.

ADAM GOPNIK

Author

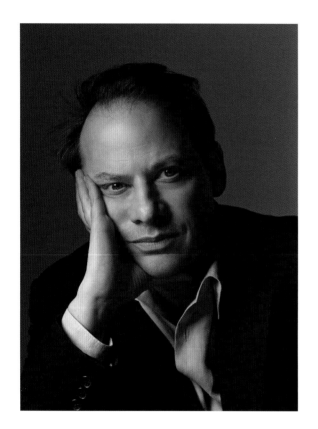

One night long ago in Paris, my wife, Martha, and I had just finished the worst day of our lives, to that point or this one. Our son Luke had been ill, and getting worse, for two days, with some kind of gastro-intestinal complaint that at first had seemed like just one of those things that happen to small kids, and then had gotten more and more severe as one day wore into the next.

We bundled him off and took him to the doctor, who—French pediatricians being less self-consciously "scientific" in affect than the American kind, more willing to be emotionally direct, sometimes alarmingly so—showed his concern. "He's very sick," he said. "We need to get him to see a surgeon immediately." The fear was that he had either appendicitis or, perhaps, a convoluted colon, or—well, I don't recall the words. I picked him up bodily and raced to the children's hospital in the 7th arrondissement, where the surgeon, just emerging from the operating room, kindly, while fighting obvious exhaustion, examined him and pronounced it nonsevere. I'll spare you all the details, but by the end of the evening, after several more taxi trips from hospital to hospital and home to pharmacy, it turned out that he had a case of salmonella poisoning—a bad case, but eminently treatable. By the time we got him home, he had taken the first dose of medicine and you could already sense his body beginning to calm and restore itself; small children are seismographs of illness—their fevers spike, their seizures can start—but they resolve themselves too, more rapidly than grown-ups do.

And so by midnight we were sure that he would be well, and, more

relieved than we have ever felt, we suddenly realized that we were hungry. But what was there in the larder to eat? Some rice, a can of beans, a handful of dried herbs, a bottle of Rhone valley red wine, some smoked *poitrine fumée*, and a few weathered apples. I put myself to work joyfully, with a glass of wine in my hand, to turn it into dinner, and I did. The results were so satisfying that, to this day, when Martha and I are exhausted or in need of comfort, I always re-produce this same dinner of improvised thanks—*profound* thanks—for a healthy child. (You can of course make this using beans-made-from-scratch, but I deeply believe that one secret of simple cooking is that no one—really no one—can tell well-rinsed canned beans of quality from the home-cooked kind.)

Spicy Rice and Beans

Serves 4

2 cloves garlic

3 strips bacon

2 tablespoons olive oil

1 teaspoon cumin seeds

¼ teaspoon cayenne, more or less

1 teaspoon sweet paprika

1 teaspoon ground turmeric

1 teaspoon kosher salt

1 cup white rice, preferably basmati

2 cups unsalted chicken stock or water

1 (14-ounce) can black beans or kidney beans, rinsed and drained

Chopped fresh herbs or tomato salsa, optional

1. Chop the garlic and bacon together. In a heavy skillet or wide pot with a cover, cook the mixture in the olive oil over medium-low heat until the garlic is just browning and the bacon begins to crisp, about 2 to 3 minutes. Add the cumin, cayenne, paprika, turmeric, and salt and stir until fragrant, about 30 seconds. Add the rice and stir until the whole thing just starts to smoke. Pour in the chicken stock or water—it should sizzle and boil. Cover, reduce the heat to low, and cook until rice is tender, 18 to 20 minutes.

2. Add the beans and fluff together with a fork. Serve with chopped fresh herbs or tomato salsa, if any is on hand.

Red Wine and Tarragon Braised Apples

Serves 4

4 apples, preferably Golden Delicious or Honeycrisp, but any kind works

2 tablespoons unsalted butter

2 tablespoons brown sugar, optional

4 sprigs fresh tarragon

1½ cups red wine, preferably a spicy Syrah

¼ cup dried cherries

1 cinnamon stick, optional

2 cloves or 1 whole star anise, optional

Crème fraîche, optional

1. Preheat the oven to 400°F.

2. Core the apples and score each with a sharp knife around the perimeter about ½ inch below the stem end. (This creates a nice puffed, architectural look when they bake.) Stick a bit of the butter, a bit of the brown sugar, and a sprig of tarragon in each core. Place in a pie plate or other small baking dish, and pour in the wine. Sprinkle the dried cherries over the wine, and place the cinnamon stick and cloves or star anise, if using them, in the dish. Bake until tender, 40 to 60 minutes.

3. These take longer to bake completely through than you might expect. Enjoy some rice and beans and conversation while you wait. Then serve the apples at once with a bit of cold crème fraîche, if you have some in the refrigerator.

SEAFOOD

MIKHAIL BARYSHNIKOV

Ballet dancer, choreographer, actor

One cool December morning in Georgia, just after dawn, I headed to the ferry dock on Cumberland Island with a fishing rod, a bucket, and a good feeling. The plan was to catch some sea trout for lunch.

I've been to this barrier island off the coast of St. Mary's many times since my first visit 40 years ago, but this time my family and I were guests of the best hosts I know, Gogo Ferguson and her husband, Dave Sayre. Meals with Gogo and Dave are big, noisy spreads where everyone pitches in. That means harvesting food right from the island. We hacked oysters from the oyster beds and pulled clams from the mud, slurping them from the shell with a squirt of Key lime.

An entire day went to slow-roasting wild boar tracked and shot with a bow and arrow commando style by one of Gogo's relatives. In other words, the pressure was on for me to hunt down lunch.

By the time I reached the dock, nature was putting on her show. Sea birds chattered and looped overhead in the rosy glow and dolphins glinted silver a few hundred yards away. The breeze was laced with salt, earth, and pine. Magic.

When the morning's first ferry pulled up with a boatload of visitors—most of Cumberland is a national park—I picked up some fishing tips from the captain, baited the hook, and let it drop into the dark water. Now, I like eating a fresh catch, but I think waiting for that tug on the line is almost as good. There's nothing to do but look out at the horizon and listen to the *lap lap* of the water. Thoughts slide in and out of your head like the tide. It's the best kind of being alone.

In about an hour I had a couple of beauties gutted, scaled, and ready to deliver triumphantly to the kitchen. We filled the insides with slices of lemon, plenty of salt, pepper, and dried oregano, then wrapped them in foil and grilled them on Dave's oyster-roasting rack over an open fire. Fresh corn, salad, and a couple of bottles of cold white wine made for one of the best fish lunches I can remember.

Many have tried to tame Cumberland by beating it back, but those meals around Gogo and Dave's big plank table remind me that embracing, even celebrating, the wildness of a place means its beauty and its secrets can be yours—at least for a little while.

Grilled Branzino with Pancetta, Lemon, and Herbs

Serves 4

6 tablespoons extra-virgin olive oil

12 thin slices of pancetta (have it sliced at the deli!)

4 branzino (about 1 pound each), gutted and scaled

Kosher salt and freshly ground black pepper

1 large lemon, thinly sliced

12 sprigs fresh thyme

8 to 12 fresh lemon verbena leaves (farmers' market or plant store)

The fresh lemon verbena in this recipe perfumes the fish with a hint of licorice and magnifies the lemon flavor.

1. Prepare a hot charcoal or gas grill fire.

2. Spread a generous amount of olive oil (about 1 tablespoon) on a 12 by 18-inch piece of heavy foil. Lay 3 slices of pancetta in a line and place one whole fish on top.

3. Season the inside of the fish with salt and pepper and stuff it with sliced lemon, several sprigs of fresh thyme, and 2 or 3 lemon verbena leaves. Rub a little olive oil on the outside of the fish (about ½ tablespoon) and sprinkle more salt and pepper on top. Wrap the fish up so it's in a little airtight package. Repeat with the other 3 fish.

4. Put all 4 fish over a hot grill fire (400°F to 500°F)—not flaming, but good and hot—then forget about them for about 15 minutes (without turning). You should hear them sizzling inside when you remove the foil packages from the grill.

5. Put the packages on a platter and let everyone open and dissect their own. If all goes well, the pancetta will be a little crisp and the fish will be flaky and infused with the lemon and herb flavors. Serve with a few simple sides, like a quinoa pilaf and fresh tomato salad. Not Cumberland, but pretty damn close.

SEAMUS MULLEN

Chef, restaurateur, cookbook author

When I was a kid, this was the first dish my grandmother Mutti taught me how to make. She inspired me to cook when I was young and eventually was the one who encouraged me to pursue cooking as a career. She recently passed away, but I will never forget my childhood memories of us together in the kitchen.

One of our favorite things to do was to pan-fry little trout that I caught in the stream that runs by our house—hence troutlings, because regardless of how big my first fish loom in my memory, Mutti never let me forget they were really cigar-size. Ideally, this dish is prepared with a whole bunch of tiny spring troutlings (6 to 7 inches long), served family style and eaten with your fingers. Otherwise, use the smallest trout you can find. If the fish are small enough, refry the bones and eat them as crispy little treats.

Mutti's Pan-Fried Troutlings

Serves 4 as a first course

4 whole brook troutlings, smallest available (3 to 6 ounces each), gutted, gills removed

Kosher salt and freshly ground black pepper

¼ cup white rice flour or chickpea flour

2 ounces (½ stick) unsalted butter

2 tablespoons capers, drained

¼ cup fresh lemon juice

3 tablespoons coarsely chopped fresh parsley

1. Season each troutling with salt and pepper on all sides, and inside the cavities as well. Put the flour on a plate and turn the troutlings in the flour to coat lightly.

2. Heat the butter in a medium-to-large cast-iron skillet (depending on the size of the fish) over medium-high heat until the foam subsides. Put the troutlings in the pan and fry on all sides until golden brown and just cooked through, 5 to 7 minutes (depending on the size of the fish). Transfer the fish with 2 spatulas to a platter or plates, add the capers and lemon juice to the pan for a few seconds, then pour the sauce over the fish and serve sprinkled with the parsley.

AMANDA FREITAG
Chef

You never know when you first meet someone who they will become in your life and how they will influence you. Robert Crosson and I met in 2008 when I took over the executive chef position at the Harrison in New York City. Robert is a ball of energy and life. When I was first introduced to him, he was painting the restaurant, then I found out he was really the bartender. He also waited on tables, cooked, ran food, expedited the kitchen line, and did pretty much anything that fell within the walls of a restaurant.

Robert has an incredible passion for food, cocktails, wine, and all things edible. He is the original foodie! So we obviously became fast friends. I love when he cooks for me, and especially when we cook together. Robert would—and still does— outwork, outparty, and outlast all of us. So, you would never know that Robert has been very ill in his life and from time to time gets worn down. He is HIV positive and has been living with his diagnosis for more than 20 years. Robert has more gusto for life than anyone I know and we should all take his example for how to live to the fullest.

Early in our friendship he told me about a time when he was very sick and homebound and he called on God's Love to bring him food. I didn't know anything about the organization and immediately wanted to learn more. As someone whose life revolves around feeding people, I was drawn to their cause.

In my family, food has always been the answer to everything, if you are happy, eat; if you are tired, eat; and, most of all, if you are sick, often nothing makes you feel better than a homemade meal.

My first visit to God's Love We Deliver on Spring Street was an emotional one. I could see and feel the commitment to caring for others that filled those hallways, and I knew right there that I had to be involved.

I have been a strong supporter of GLWD ever since and have done many projects and campaigns with them over the years. I believe that food heals and that with one simple handshake and a shared meal, you can make someone well again and have a forever friend.

Salmon Fillet with Salsa Verde and Farro Salad

Serves 4

1½ cups farro

4 cups water

1 teaspoon kosher salt, more for seasoning the farro

¼ cup olive oil

4 (6-ounce) salmon fillets with skin

½ teaspoon freshly ground black pepper

2 cups arugula

½ cup salsa verde (see below)

1 lemon

SALSA VERDE

2 cloves garlic, peeled

2 anchovy fillets

½ teaspoon kosher salt

1 tablespoon Dijon mustard

½ cup coarsely chopped fresh chives

½ cup coarsely chopped fresh flat-leaf parsley

2 tablespoons coarsely chopped fresh oregano

¼ teaspoon dried red pepper flakes

½ cup extra-virgin olive oil

½ cup canola oil

Freshly ground black pepper

1. To make the salsa verde, use both the blade edge and flat side of a chef's knife to mince and mash the garlic, anchovies, and salt to a paste. Stir in the mustard. Transfer the paste to a food processor, add the herbs and red pepper flakes, and pulse while slowly drizzling in the oils. The consistency should be chunky. Season with salt and pepper and set aside.

2. Preheat the oven to 350°F.

3. Put the farro and water in a saucepan and bring to a boil over medium-high heat. Reduce the heat and simmer, covered, until al dente, 20 to 30 minutes. Drain off any excess water and transfer to a bowl. Season with salt.

4. Heat the olive oil in a large oven-safe skillet over high heat. Pat the salmon dry and season with 1 teaspoon of the salt and the pepper. Cook the fillets in the skillet skin side down for 2 minutes. Transfer the pan to the oven and bake the salmon, still skin side down, until the skin is crisp and golden but the flesh is still just translucent in the center, about 5 minutes.

5. To serve, divide the arugula among 4 plates; top with the salmon, skin side up. Sprinkle about ¼ cup of the farro over each and drizzle generously with the salsa verde (about 2 tablespoons per plate). Halve the lemon, remove the seeds, and squeeze the juice over the salsa verde.

STANLEY TUCCI

Actor, director, writer, author

After immigrating to America, my mother's family settled in Verplanck, New York, a small town on the Hudson River. In the back of their modest house was a sizeable garden in which they not only grew everything imaginable, but where they raised rabbits, chickens, and the occasional goat or two; all of which were used to sustain a growing family.

Being so near the river they were also able to cull its edible riches to add to their table. As a boy I loved going to the Hudson with my grandparents, tying pieces of raw chicken to the bottoms of crab nets and lowering them off the end of an abandoned steamboat dock into the green-brown waters. By late afternoon we would be devouring a bevy of boiled crabs accompanied by corn on the cob, boiled potatoes, tomato salad, and my grandmother's homemade bread.

The feast was served on a newspaper-covered table nestled beneath a grapevine-wrapped trellis. If my uncle Tony and aunt Grace had recently returned from Cape Cod, we would be treated to their catch of fresh clams on the half shell and bluefish. All of this, followed by a boisterous game of bocce, made for what are now much missed seafood-filled summer days.

Baked Bluefish

Serves 4

1 (3-pound) whole bluefish, butterflied, without bones, head, or tail

Kosher salt and freshly ground black pepper

2 tablespoons freshly squeezed lemon juice

1 cup fresh bread crumbs

3 cloves garlic, finely chopped

2 tablespoons chopped fresh flat-leaf parsley

½ cup olive oil

2 lemons, 1 sliced into thin rounds, the other cut into wedges for serving

1. Preheat the oven to 350°F.

2. Line a rimmed baking pan with foil. Put the butterflied fish, flesh side up, on the pan, season with salt and pepper, and sprinkle with the lemon juice.

3. In a bowl, combine the bread crumbs, garlic, parsley, and a pinch each of salt and pepper, and gradually add the oil, stirring with a fork. Evenly spread the bread-crumb mixture over the fish and arrange the lemon slices on top.

4. Bake until the fish just flakes, 20 to 30 minutes, then broil the fish until slightly brown, about 1 minute. Serve with the lemon wedges.

ZARELA MARTINEZ
Chef, author

When I was a young girl, I asked my mother why she named me Zarela instead of giving me a "normal" name. She answered, "Because it will look good in lights." We lived on a cattle ranch in Chihuahua state in Mexico, five hours away from any city. I was a tomboy who tamed horses, branded and neutered the calves at round-up time, and went on cattle drives on my cutting horse, Desprecio, so it's always been a mystery what it is she saw in me that inspired her to make that statement. But I do know that she did everything to make it possible.

I was married to a widower with three children and working as a social worker in El Paso, Texas, when I got pregnant with twins. I started baking and selling Christmas cookies and cooking for family and friends to make extra money, when Mother decided that I should become a caterer. She found Lillian Haines,

a well-known Beverly Hills caterer, and booked a private one-week course for me to learn the ins and outs of the business. Other courses would follow, but in the meantime, she started going on recipe-hunting expeditions to Mexico for me.

This red-snapper hash recipe, one of her best finds, became my signature dish. It was inspired by a *botana* (snack to accompany drinks, like the Spanish *tapas*) that she and my stepfather had at a bar in Tampico located opposite a cemetery. The bar had a sign in the window that read, *Se esta mejor aqui que en frente*—"You rest better here than across the street." Another posted notice advised that neither women nor military personnel were allowed inside. So my stepfather had to buy the *botanas* and beer, and they ate outside together, sitting on the back of their pickup truck with a beautiful view of the cemetery.

Salpicón de Huachinango (Red Snapper Hash)

Serves 6 to 8 as an appetizer, more as taco filling

4 ounces (1 stick) unsalted butter

3 tablespoons minced garlic (6 large cloves)

1 cup minced scallions (6 or 7)

2½ cups chopped ripe tomatoes (about 3 medium)

3 fresh jalapeño or serrano peppers, finely chopped, with seeds

2 teaspoons ground cumin

1½ teaspoons freshly ground Mexican (Ceylon) cinnamon

½ teaspoon ground cloves

½ teaspoon kosher salt, more for seasoning

2½ pounds red snapper fillets, skinned

Warm, freshly made corn tortillas or crisp-fried tortilla chips

1. In a large heavy skillet over medium heat, melt 2 ounces of the butter until the foam subsides. Add 1½ tablespoons of the minced garlic and cook, stirring, until fragrant, about 1 minute. Add the scallions and cook, stirring, 1 minute longer. Add the tomatoes, peppers, spices, and about ½ teaspoon salt and cook, stirring often, until the sauce is concentrated slightly, about 5 minutes.

2. Cut the fish fillets into halves or several large pieces, depending on size. Season them with salt and place them over the sauce in the pan in 1 layer (work in 2 batches, if necessary). Adjust the heat to maintain a low simmer. Poach the fish, uncovered, just until the flesh begins to turn opaque, about 1 minute. Carefully turn the fillets over with two spatulas and poach on the other side until slightly undercooked (they will be cooked further later), about 1 minute more. Transfer the fish to a plate to cool and repeat with a second batch of fish, if necessary.

3. Pour the fish sauce into a large bowl. Shred the fish, removing any bones, and add it to the sauce. (The salpicón can be prepared up to this point several hours ahead and refrigerated.)

4. In the cleaned skillet, heat the remaining 2 ounces of butter over medium heat until hot and bubbling. Add the remaining 1½ tablespoons of garlic and cook, stirring, until fragrant, about 1 minute. Add the shredded fish and sauce and cook, stirring occasionally, just until heated through, about 5 minutes. Transfer to a serving bowl and serve immediately with warm, freshly made corn tortillas or crisp-fried tortilla chips.

JORDAN FROSOLONE
Chef

For as long as I can remember, I have been an Italophile. There's something about their culture, design aesthetic, and culinary traditions that has always drawn me in. When I was younger I loved hearing stories from my Sicilian grandmother about what it was like to grow up, the daughter of a fishmonger, in Chicago after her parents immigrated to the United States.

Because of her memories and my subsequent travels to Sicily, I have come to believe that the culture and food there is truly unique to that island, even compared with anything else in Italy. I did not have many opportunities to cook for my grandmother, but the occasion I remember most fondly was when I made her

braised rabbit in my very small apartment in Chicago, at the start of my cooking career. I will always have the vivid memory of watching her eat with her hands and commenting about how she used to eat rabbit all the time as a little girl. She also talked about how, when she was growing up, she and her family would eat "off cuts" of meat, offal, pasta, and, because of the family business, a lot of seafood.

Much of Sicilian cuisine is historically marine and vegetable based. This has led to the development of some of the most vibrant and abundant fish and vegetable markets in the world. One such market exists on the historical island of Ortigia, in the beautiful city of Siracusa. On a trip to Sicily in spring 2005, my dear friend Luca DiLuciano brought me to this market, where we took our pick of all the best seafood and produce. These ingredients served as inspiration for my first Sicilian Easter feast, which naturally included a traditional dish of seafood and couscous.

Seafood Couscous

Serves 4

⅔ cup couscous

½ teaspoon kosher salt, more for seasoning

¾ cup boiling water

Finely grated zest of 2 lemons

Finely grated zest of 2 limes

2 fresh or jarred Calabrian chilies or other small red chilies, thinly sliced

½ cup plus 1 tablespoon extra-virgin olive oil, more for grilling

12 ounces cleaned squid

12 ounces large shrimp (26 to 30 per pound), peeled and deveined

10 ounces baby octopus, beak removed

Freshly ground black pepper

1¼ pounds cherry tomatoes, halved

10 ounces shelled fresh or thawed peas

1 medium fennel bulb (about 8 ounces), trimmed, cored, and thinly sliced (about 2½ cups)

⅔ cup sliced almonds, toasted

2 tablespoons coarsely chopped fresh basil

2 tablespoons coarsely chopped fresh mint

¼ cup drained capers

¼ cup fresh lemon juice

This delicious main course salad is served at room temperature, so many of the elements can be prepared an hour or two ahead. Toss together within a half hour of serving.

1. Prepare a medium-hot grill fire or heat a griddle over medium-high heat.

2. Put the couscous in a large bowl, sprinkle with the kosher salt and pour the boiling water over it. Let stand 5 minutes. Fluff with a fork. Reserve.

3. Combine the lemon and lime zest in a medium bowl with the chilies and ½ cup of the olive oil.

4. Season the seafood with salt and pepper and toss with a drizzle of olive oil. If using a grill, skewer the shrimp. Place the calamari, shrimp, and octopus on the grill or griddle, turning once you have a good sear, until lightly cooked through, about 2 minutes for the calamari and shrimp and 4 minutes for the octopus. Remove from heat and cut the calamari and octopus into rings or bite-size pieces. Add the seafood to the marinade, preferably while still hot. Marinate for at least 20 minutes, stirring occasionally.

5. Heat the remaining tablespoon of olive oil in a large skillet over medium-high heat until shimmering hot. Add the tomatoes and sauté until blistered, 6 to 7 minutes. Set aside.

6. Cook the peas in boiling water until tender, 2 to 5 minutes, then drain and put in a bowl of ice water to stop cooking. When cool, drain and set aside.

7. Add the fennel, toasted almonds, peas, tomatoes, basil, and mint to the couscous and toss to combine. Add the shrimp, calamari, and octopus, with as much of the marinade as you like, and toss to combine. Add the capers and lemon juice, combine, and adjust the seasoning as needed. Serve at room temperature.

ANITA LO

Chef, restaurateur

When I was little, I spent several summers on Cape Cod with my family. There I learned to dig for steamer clams. We'd take the day's harvest and place them in clean seawater sprinkled with cornmeal and let them spit the sand overnight. The next day for dinner, my mother would cook the clams in a pot in a shallow puddle of boiling water. We would eat piles of them, pulling off their skins, rinsing them in their own hot broth, and finally dipping them in melted butter before popping them in our mouths. After that we'd have steamed lobsters with more drawn butter, corn on the cob, baked potatoes, and salad.

We stopped going to Cape Cod when I was about seven, but thereafter I asked for this meal every year for my birthday dinner. When I was 15, I didn't get along with my stepfather and was sent away to boarding school. It was a scary transition. But the first day of orientation, the school had a clambake. I hadn't had steamer clams in a long time and the sweet, salty flavors made me feel like I belonged. Years later, I discovered a steamer-clam bed near my then new house on Long Island, and again it was like a homecoming. This dish is one of the first meals I prepared for my 2-year-old niece when she first visited my restaurant Annisa. I like to think I was passing on a sense of place, of identity, and of caring.

Lobster and Clams with Corn

Serves 2

2 (1-pound) lobsters

12 steamer clams

2 ears corn, shucked; kernels cut off cobs

2 ounces (½ stick) unsalted butter, chilled, cut into pieces

1 teaspoon thinly sliced chives

½ teaspoon chopped fresh tarragon

Kosher salt and freshly ground black pepper

1 lemon, halved, seeds removed

1. Bring 1 inch of seawater or well-salted water to a boil in a large pot. Add the lobsters, cover the pot, and steam for 8 minutes. Remove the lobsters to a cutting board, let cool slightly, then remove the shells and cut the meat into large pieces. Discard the cooking liquid.

2. Rinse and scrub the clams. Put in a pot with ½ cup water, cover, and steam over medium-high heat until the clams open, 5 to 8 minutes. Remove the clams, reserving the liquid. Shell the clams and remove the skins from the necks. Set aside. Strain the clam cooking liquid through a damp-paper-towel-lined sieve set over a bowl and reserve.

3. Put the clam cooking liquid in a skillet, add the corn kernels, and bring to a boil over medium-high heat. Add the butter and swirl the pan until the butter is incorporated and the mixture is creamy. Remove from the heat. With a slotted spoon, remove the corn to 2 heated wide bowls, stir in the chives and tarragon to the corn mixture, and season with salt and pepper. Keep warm.

4. Add the lobster pieces to the sauce and reheat, covered, over low heat, about 2 minutes. Add the cleaned clams and reheat 1 minute more. Season with salt, pepper, and lemon juice, and spoon the seafood and sauce over the corn. Serve immediately.

JOAN RIVERS
Entertainer

When I first got married, I wanted to be all things: a superwoman, an Amazon woman, the Spartan woman who said, "Come back with your shield or on it." Meaning, I wanted to be a great wife, a great mother, a great housekeeper, a great cook, a great entertainer—a great everything!

On the same night I was to appear on *The Ed Sullivan Show*, I decided to host my first real dinner party in New York, and I was determined to make one of my favorite dishes: lobster thermidor. All day long, I prepared dinner for my guests. We sat down, the meal was served, and we ate. I thought I was such a great cook and I was impressed that I could do it all without any help. It was a warm December night, so after dinner one of my guests suggested that we go for a walk to look at the city's amazing Christmas decorations. On our way home, we passed by a delicatessen and my guests suggested we go in. Once inside, they ordered major sandwiches, which they wolfed down. This told me that my lobster thermidor was far from the success I thought it was. When I got home, I noticed that there was a lot of garbage from dinner that even our dog turned down.

That night, my husband, Edgar, said to me, "Why don't you just admit it? You're a great writer, you're a great performer, but get out of the kitchen." And that was the last time I tried to cook something…anything. It was 1971 when I walked out of the kitchen, and I have never since gone back in. So, this recipe for lobster thermidor technically isn't mine, but the amazing one of a great caterer whom I've used ever since that fateful night.

Lobster Thermidor

Serves 4 as a main course or 8 as a first course

4 (1½-pound) live lobsters

3 ounces (6 tablespoons) unsalted butter

8 ounces white mushrooms, trimmed and quartered

1 cup heavy cream

4 large egg yolks

2 tablespoons medium-dry sherry

1 tablespoon Dijon mustard

1 tablespoon Worcestershire sauce

1½ teaspoons Maggi seasoning

½ teaspoon Tabasco sauce

2 teaspoons kosher salt

1 teaspoon freshly ground black pepper

Half roasted red bell pepper, deveined, seeded, and diced

3 tablespoons chopped fresh parsley

½ cup soft fresh bread crumbs

½ ounce finely grated fresh Parmesan (½ cup using a rasp grater)

1. Boil or steam the lobsters in a large pot until they turn completely red and are just cooked through, 10 to 12 minutes.

2. Halve the bodies with a large knife and twist off and crack the claws. Remove the meat from the tails and claws and cut into small pieces. Clean out and discard other matter from the shells and arrange them, open side up, on a large rimmed baking sheet.

3. Heat 2 tablespoons of the butter in a skillet over medium-high heat and cook the mushrooms, stirring, until tender and lightly browned, about 7 minutes. Transfer to a plate and let cool.

4. Set a fine- or medium-mesh sieve over a large bowl. Heat the cream in a small saucepan over medium heat. Whisk the egg yolks in a small bowl and slowly whisk the hot cream into the yolks. Return the yolk mixture to the saucepan and cook, stirring with a wooden spoon over medium-low heat until it begins to thicken and coats the spoon (do not let boil or the mixture will curdle).

5. Immediately pour the cream mixture through the sieve into the large bowl. Let cool.

6. Preheat the oven to 400°F and put a rack in the upper third of the oven.

7. Stir the sherry, mustard, Worcestershire sauce, Maggi, Tabasco, salt, and pepper into the cooled cream sauce. Then stir in the lobster, mushrooms, pepper, and 1 tablespoon of the parsley. Adjust the seasoning and fill the lobster shells with the mixture.

8. In a bowl, combine the bread crumbs, grated cheese, and remaining 2 tablespoons of parsley and sprinkle over the lobster mixture. Melt the remaining 4 tablespoons of butter and drizzle over the crumbs.

9. Bake the lobsters until golden and heated through, 8 to 10 minutes. If not brown enough, transfer to the broiler and broil until golden brown, about 2 minutes. Serve immediately.

Editor's note: *The lobsters can be completely prepared up to 2 hours ahead and refrigerated until ready to bake. Cold lobsters may take a little longer to heat through.*

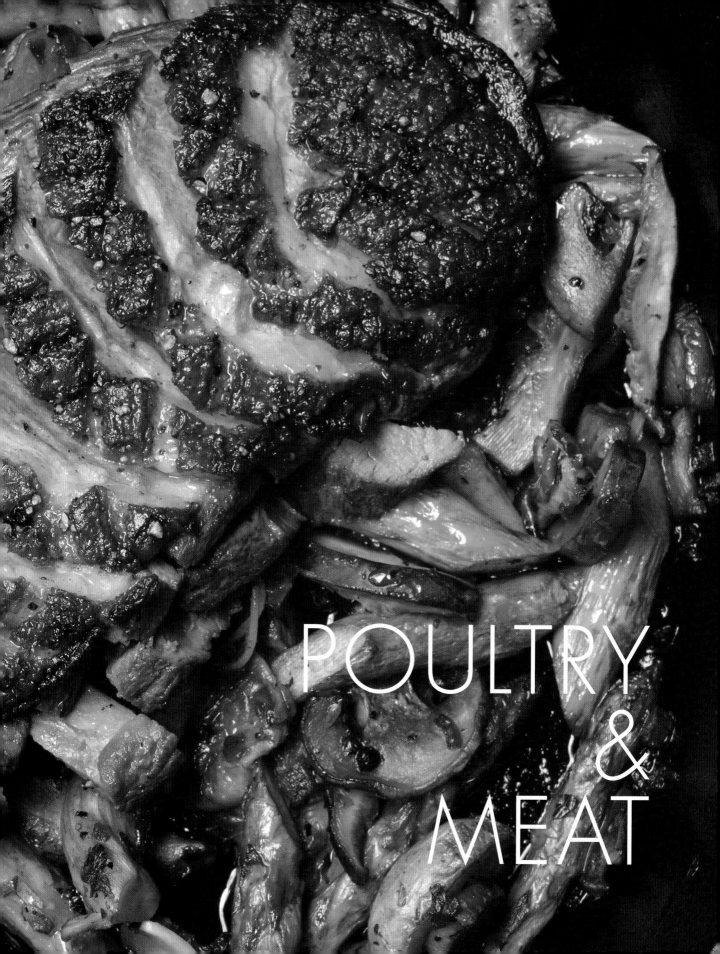

POULTRY
&
MEAT

INA GARTEN
Cookbook author, television host

Cooking, for me, is about connecting with people. When I cook, everyone shows up, and that's exactly what I love about cooking. I want my friends to think that dinner is something I just whipped up in the few minutes before they arrived, but between you and me, it's a lot of work—shopping, cooking, serving, and finally cleaning up at midnight! But the conversations that we have around the kitchen table are the glue that holds us together, and for me, it's worth all the trouble.

One dinner that I'll always remember is the one I made for Adam Gopnik and Richard Avedon, who were each other's best friends. Adam is an amazing writer and cook, and since he was living in Paris, I wanted to honor him with a truly American dinner. Nothing is more American than Thanksgiving, but the dinner was in the spring, so I asked myself, "Wouldn't that be odd?" I realized

that yes, it would be odd, but that's exactly what would also make it surprising. And since Thanksgiving is everyone's favorite meal, it would be perfect.

The real secret is that roast turkey is one of the easiest meals I make. I roast it the way I roast a chicken, with the vegetables right in the pan—big wedges of fennel, carrots, onions, and potatoes—so you have a whole meal in one pan. That night with Adam and Richard, I set the table in the kitchen so I could carve the turkey and still be at the party. It was one of the most magical evenings I can remember—not only because the guests were so special, but also because the meal was relaxed and fun.

I guess my dinner was a success, because Adam emailed me from Paris to say that he'd given his wife, Martha, who unfortunately hadn't been able to join us, a bite-by-bite description of the meal. He said she was so annoyed

and jealous that she made him sleep on the sofa that night. I know he was kidding, but it was such a charming way to say thank you. To this day, this memory reminds me that cooking isn't about impressing people but rather about bringing them together and making them feel good. If I'm having a difficult week, am under the weather, or simply feeling far from home, a good dinner with friends always heals my soul.

Perfect Roast Turkey

From *Barefoot Contessa Parties!*

Serves 8

1 (12-pound) fresh turkey, preferably organic

Kosher salt and freshly ground black pepper

1 large bunch of fresh thyme

1 lemon, halved

3 large Spanish onions

1 head garlic, halved crosswise

2 ounces (½ stick), unsalted butter, melted

½ cup extra-virgin olive oil

8 carrots, peeled and cut into 2-inch chunks

10 red new potatoes, halved

3 medium heads fennel, stalks and fronds removed, cut into wedges through the core

Remember how your mother used to get up at 4am on Thanksgiving so she could put the turkey in the oven to roast for 10 hours? Then she had to baste it all day to keep it from drying out, which, of course, it did anyway? Forget it. A 12- to 15-pound turkey cooks in 2½ to 3 hours, and you let it rest for at least 20 minutes before you carve it. Everyone will say, "This is the best turkey I ever ate." I use an organic turkey whenever I can.

1. Preheat the oven to 350°F.

2. Take the giblets out of the turkey and wash the turkey inside and out. Remove any excess fat and leftover pinfeathers and pat the outside dry. Place the turkey in a large roasting pan. Liberally salt and pepper the inside of the cavity. Stuff the cavity with the thyme; lemon halves; one of the onions, peeled and quartered; and garlic. Brush the outside of the turkey with the butter and sprinkle with salt and pepper. Tie the legs together with string and tuck the wing tips under the body. Peel, halve, and slice the remaining onions, toss them with ¼ cup of the olive oil, and scatter them around the turkey.

3. Roast the turkey for 1 hour. Toss the carrots, potatoes, and fennel with the remaining ¼ cup of olive oil and add to the roasting pan. Continue to roast for about 1½ hours, or until the juices run clear when you cut between the leg and the body.

4. Remove the turkey to a cutting board and cover with aluminum foil; let rest for 20 minutes.

5. Meanwhile, stir the vegetables and return the pan to the oven. Continue to cook the vegetables while the turkey rests.

6. Slice the turkey and serve on a platter with the roasted vegetables and pan juices.

LIDIA BASTIANICH

Chef, restaurateur

I had a very close relationship with my grandmother Rosa as a young girl. I spent most of my free time—vacations, weekends, even after-school hours—in her small courtyard not too far from Pula, Istria. My earliest and fondest memories are of helping my grandmother in the garden as I walked behind her while she hoed up the potatoes for the next planting. On market days I would pick the vegetables with her early in the morning, wash them in the courtyard, and load them into my grandmother's handcart. Once at the market, I helped her weigh the vegetables and put them in paper cones for customers. On the way home, we would barter whatever we hadn't sold for old restaurant bread, which we fed to our animals.

Displaced from Istria, our family had been living in a political refugee camp outside of Trieste for two years before Catholic Charities brought us to New York in 1958. My mother, called Grandma Erminia in our family, came to the United States with my father, my brother Franco, and me, when I was only 11 years old. Soon after our arrival, we moved to North Bergen, New Jersey, where my father took a job as a mechanic at a Chevrolet plant. However, as more displaced Istrians arrived in the States, the five boroughs of New York City became the focus for the formation of our ethnic communities, and so we moved to such a neighborhood, in Astoria, Queens.

Grandma Erminia came to live with me when my children were small and helped take care of them while we were running our first restaurants. Chicken and potatoes, cooked together in a

big cast-iron skillet until they're crisp and moist at the same time, is my mother's specialty. Growing up, my brother and I demanded this dish every week; a generation later, our kids—Tanya, Joe, Eric, Paul, and Estelle—clamored for it too. And now a new generation of little ones is asking their great-grandmother to make chicken and potatoes for them. This is by far one of our most requested recipes; I am sure Grandma's personality must have something to do with it, but the tasty dish has merits all its own.

Pollo e Patate della Mamma (My Mother's Chicken and Potatoes)

Serves 4 as a main course or 8 as a first course

6 strips thin-sliced bacon

2½ pounds chicken thighs and drumsticks, rinsed, dried, and excess skin and fat removed

1¼ teaspoons kosher salt, more or less as desired

½ cup canola oil

1 pound 1½- to 2-inch red bliss potatoes

3 tablespoons extra-virgin olive oil

2 medium onions, peeled and quartered lengthwise

2 short branches of fresh rosemary with plenty of needles

1 or 2 (or more!) sweet or hot pickled cherry peppers, halved and seeded

1. Break 4 to 6 toothpicks into 1-inch pieces. Cut the bacon strips in half crosswise and roll each into a neat, tight cylinder. Stick a piece of toothpick through each roll to secure it.

2. Heat the canola oil in a large, deep skillet over high heat until shimmering hot. Sprinkle the chicken on all sides with 1 teaspoon of the salt. Working in batches, fry the chicken along with the bacon rolls, without crowding the pan, until the chicken is browned on all sides and the bacon rolls are starting to crisp, 7 to 10 minutes per batch. Transfer each batch of fried chicken and bacon to a large bowl. When all the chicken has been cooked, pour off the frying oil in the pan.

3. Meanwhile, rinse and dry the potatoes, slice each one in half along its longest axis (yielding the largest cut surface area), and put in a bowl with the olive oil and the remaining ¼ teaspoon salt. Toss to coat.

4. Return the skillet to medium heat and put all the potatoes, cut side down, in a single layer in the pan, pouring the olive oil into the skillet with them. Cook the potatoes without moving until they form a crust, about 4 minutes. Then move them around the pan, still cut side down, to brown evenly, if necessary. Turn them over to brown their rounded sides, about 2 minutes.

5. Tuck the onion wedges, rosemary branches, and hot pickled cherry peppers between the potatoes, then return the chicken pieces and bacon rolls to the pan along with any juices from the bowl (if there are no juices, add ¼ cup water). Cover and cook over medium-low to medium heat, tossing the ingredients and spreading them out two or three times, and shaking the pan occasionally, until the chicken is just cooked through, 20 to 25 minutes.

6. Remove the cover, toss and spread out the ingredients again, and cook, uncovered, until the juices have reduced to a glaze and the chicken and bacon are nicely caramelized. Season with salt and serve in the skillet.

DANIEL BOULUD

Chef, restaurateur

Tagine is a dish I have made many times and love to make because I can be creative and seasonal with it. It was first prepared for me by an old friend, Baby Dahan, and to this day, it reminds me of close family ties and great friendships. It's the perfect meal to make for someone who needs comfort, because to me, it is simply heartwarming. It is also my wife's favorite. I don't know if it's the juiciness of the tender chicken or the intoxicating aroma of North-African spices, but whenever we are cooking at home together, it's what we crave.

The important thing with this recipe is to have a good spice mix and to let the tagine cook slowly and gently. After that, I like to add vegetables that are in season, and sometimes different dried fruits or olive varieties, just for fun. For example, during the summer, I might use eggplant instead of cauliflower; during the winter, perhaps parsnips and turnips. But whatever the season, it's really the spice mix that makes the flavor so warm and nourishing.

The tagine is not just a dish for two; it's also perfect to feed a crowd. I like

to serve it in the tagine, or pot, in which it was baked with a big bowl of fluffy couscous on the side and a large serving spoon. It's a very unpretentious way to create a little show for your guests: simply set the pot on the table, remove the lid, and watch their faces light up when they catch the escaping spice-scented steam. After that, no one can resist. Whether it's with family or friends, just be sure to enjoy this dish in good company.

Chicken Tagine

Serves 2 to 4

1 (2½-pound) farm-raised chicken

2 tablespoons tagine spice mix (see below), more for sauce

1 teaspoon kosher salt, more for seasoning

6 tablespoons olive oil

3 large plum tomatoes

1 small head cauliflower, cut into bite-size florets

1 large onion, diced

3 cloves garlic, minced

1 tablespoon finely grated peeled fresh ginger

1 pinch saffron

1 tablespoon tomato paste

2 cups unsalted chicken stock

3 tablespoons sliced preserved lemon, rind only

1 cup Castelvetrano olives

Freshly ground black pepper

½ cup cilantro leaves

TAGINE SPICE MIX

3 tablespoons coriander seeds

2 cinnamon sticks, broken in half

¾ teaspoon cardamom pods

1¾ teaspoons whole allspice

3½ tablespoons sweet paprika

1 tablespoon plus ½ teaspoon ground turmeric

1 tablespoon powdered ginger

1 teaspoon garlic powder

½ teaspoon ground nutmeg

ACCOMPANIMENT

Couscous or basmati rice

1. To prepare the tagine spice mix, toast the whole spices over low heat in a large dry sauté pan, stirring, until fragrant. Transfer to a clean coffee/spice grinder and grind to a powder. Transfer to a bowl and stir in the remaining spices. Store in a covered container.

2. When ready to make the tagine, butcher the chicken into legs, thighs, and breast halves with wings attached, then halve breast pieces again, for breast quarters. Remove the wing tips and the bones from the thighs. Rub the chicken pieces all over with 2 tablespoons of the tagine spice mix, ½ teaspoon of the salt, and 3 tablespoons of the olive oil. Let stand while preparing the vegetables.

3. Bring a large pot of salted water to a boil and set a bowl of ice water on the side. Core the tomatoes and score an X on each end. Boil the tomatoes for 20 seconds and then transfer to the ice water to stop cooking. Boil the cauliflower florets for 3 minutes and then transfer to the ice water to stop cooking. Drain and pat dry.

4. Peel the skins from the tomatoes. Cut into quarters lengthwise and trim away the seeds to make petals.

5. Preheat the oven to 350°F.

6. Heat the remaining 3 tablespoons of olive oil in a large skillet over medium heat. Brown the chicken in batches, starting skin side down, until lightly browned all over. Transfer to a large tagine or 5-quart Dutch oven. Add the cauliflower to the skillet and cook, stirring occasionally, until golden. Transfer to the pot with the chicken. Reduce the heat to medium low, add the diced onion, garlic, ginger, saffron, remaining ½ teaspoon of salt, and a pinch more of the spice mix. Cook, stirring, until the onion is translucent, 3 to 5 minutes. Stir in the tomato paste and chicken stock and simmer until reduced by one-third.

7. Pour the sauce over the chicken. Cover, transfer to the oven, and braise for 20 minutes. Stir in the tomato petals, preserved lemon rind, and olives; braise until the chicken is cooked through, about 20 minutes more. Season with salt and pepper.

8. Garnish the chicken with cilantro leaves and serve it in the tagine, with couscous or basmati rice on the side.

ALICE WATERS
Chef, restaurateur, activist, author

I have always thought that one of the greatest foods in existence is garlic. So much so that in the very early days of Chez Panisse, we started a yearly garlic festival. We've always held the festival on Bastille Day—July 14—and it's a wonderful midsummer celebration of music, dance, wine, and everything that is ripe and in season—and of the garlic harvest. A lot of garlic it is: early in the morning on Bastille Day every year, four or five women from the neighborhood arrive, gather around a table in the dining room, and start helping to peel the cloves. We call them our garlic ladies, and some of them have been coming for the better part of 40 years! By the afternoon they have peeled hundreds upon hundreds of cloves—all of which are then handily dispatched by the cooks and put to good use for that night's dinner. The entire restaurant is festooned with beribboned garlands of garlic, including one in the shape of a giant peace sign that presides over the entrance. You can imagine the aroma!

One year, in the late seventies, right after we started the festival, the great filmmaker Les Blank brought his camera and made his documentary *Garlic Is as Good as Ten Mothers*—the title comes from an amazing old proverb that I love. One of the dishes Les filmed us preparing was a roasted chicken with 40 cloves of garlic. I remember it was one of the first times I had made it, but I thought it would perfectly reflect the incredible richness and flavor of garlic—and show just how much of it you can use. Les's documentary is wonderful, but when I saw the film later on, I realized I hadn't cooked the garlic or the chicken nearly as much as I should have! The way I prepared chicken back then has absolutely nothing to do with the way we cook it now. (Now we often spit-roast it over the fire, though turning it in a hot cast-iron pan or in the oven can be just as good.)

That is part of the beauty of cooking. It's about doing it over and over to get it right, year after year, learning from other cooks and friends, and improving

and changing as you go. And, of course, it is also about *enjoying* that evolution of taste, company, and conversations along the way.

We have learned so much now: it has been almost four decades since the first festival, and many thousands of garlicky chickens have been roasted since I blithely made it for Les Blank. And this year for Bastille Day, chicken with 40 cloves of garlic—cooked just the way we like it these days—is exactly what we are making.

Chicken with 40 Cloves of Garlic

Adapted from *The Art of Simple Food II*

Serves 4

4 chicken legs or 1 whole chicken cut up into 8 pieces

Kosher salt and freshly ground black pepper

5 tablespoons extra-virgin olive oil

4 heads garlic, separated into cloves, unpeeled

10 thyme sprigs or 5 savory sprigs

1 bay leaf

4 thick slices crusty bread

1. Season the chicken with salt and pepper and let stand 30 minutes.

2. Preheat the oven to 375°F.

3. Heat a large heavy skillet over medium-high heat. Pat the seasoned chicken dry. Add 2 tablespoons of the olive oil to the skillet and swirl to coat the bottom. Add the chicken and brown on both sides, about 16 minutes total.

4. Meanwhile, put the garlic cloves, herb sprigs, and bay leaf in a low ovenproof pot or casserole with a cover, and toss with the remaining 3 tablespoons of olive oil.

5. Arrange the chicken in one layer over the garlic, cover the surface of the chicken with a round of parchment or foil to help keep the juices in, and cover the pot with a tight-fitting lid.

6. Bake the chicken in the middle of the oven until just cooked through, 45 to 50 minutes. Remove from the oven.

7. Turn the broiler on high. Remove the lid and the parchment from the chicken and put under the broiler until the chicken is browned, about 5 minutes. Remove.

8. Put the bread on a rimmed baking sheet and broil until toasted, about 1 minute per side.

9. Serve the chicken and garlic with the toasted bread.

CHARLIE PALMER
Chef

I've worked in plenty of kitchens over the years—some truly magnificent, others only makeshift—and I've turned out plenty of good meals from both. But the best meals I can remember were those I had outdoors; whether I cooked them there or only served them there, they're the meals that stick with me.

It's anyone's guess why cooking and eating in the open air makes food taste better. Maybe it's in our DNA—hunting and gathering is as old as mankind. When I was growing up in rural New York State, I was told that nature is good for the soul. And I still believe it. So I've continued to enjoy the outdoor life, and I've taught my four boys to do the same. Whether we're hunting, camping, or just taking time out from modern life, eating outdoors is a family ritual we like to share with our friends. Hunters and anglers, or hikers and foragers, we all find that it's the time spent together that makes our campfire meals more rewarding.

Duck hunting is a family activity for us. Together we catch our food, together we prepare it, and together we cook it. There's something so primal about sitting down for a just-caught meal—whether it's around a makeshift campfire or our kitchen table at home. You know the source of the food you're enjoying and that it's at its absolute freshest. Plus, food has always been a centrifugal force: bringing people together for conversation and laughter since the beginning of time.

Duck Breast with Wild Mushrooms and Asparagus

Adapted from *Remington Camp Cooking* by Charlie Palmer

Serves 2 generously

4 wild duck breasts, boneless, skin on, about 1⅓ pounds total, or 1 large moulard (domestic) duck breast, about 1 pound

Kosher salt and freshly ground black pepper

8 small new potatoes, halved (8 ounces total)

8 spears asparagus, trimmed, cut into 1-inch segments (6 ounces total)

6 ounces mixed wild mushrooms (morel, shiitake caps, hen of the woods), sliced or torn

½ cup chopped red onion

1 large clove garlic, sliced

1 teaspoon fresh thyme leaves

When using true wild duck, like mallard or field duck, you will need 2 whole breasts per person. Care must be taken not to overcook wild duck (nothing past medium) or you will get that dry, liverlike taste. You may also have to wash the pan with bacon fat or vegetable oil to keep the breast moist. If cooking wild duck, I suggest cutting the breast in ½-inch slices before serving, whereas with domestic duck, you don't need to do that. The wild duck is a lot tougher and will need a steak knife as opposed to a table knife.

1. Preheat the oven to 350°F.

2. Score the skin of the duck in a crosshatch pattern to release the maximum amount of fat. Season each breast with salt and plenty of freshly ground black pepper (much will fall off during the cooking process).

3. Put the duck breasts, skin side down, in an unheated 10-inch cast-iron skillet (or other ovenproof heavy skillet). Put the skillet over medium heat and cook until the skin is well browned and crisp, 7 to 10 minutes. If using a large moulard duck breast, transfer the skillet to the oven and continue to cook, skin side up, 5 minutes.

4. Transfer the duck from the pan to a plate and set aside. Add the potatoes, cut side down, to the hot fat and transfer the pan to the oven. Roast until the potatoes are just tender, about 15 minutes. Leave the oven on.

5. Return the pan to the stovetop over medium-high heat and stir in the remaining ingredients, ½ teaspoon salt, and ¼ teaspoon pepper. Sauté until the mushrooms begin to color and all of the ingredients are hot, 3 to 5 minutes.

6. Return the duck breasts, skin side up, to the pan and pour in any juices left on the plate. Place the skillet in the oven to roast all of the ingredients together for 10 minutes.

7. Remove the pan from the oven and let sit for a few minutes to allow the duck breasts to rest before slicing and serving.

Editor's note: *Charlie Palmer cooks his duck breasts in a heated skillet, but for the home cook without a heady exhaust fan, starting with a cold pan helps render the fat and cook the duck breast without producing nearly as much smoke.*

DANNY MEYER

Restaurateur

I was born with a voracious appetite. Like many other growing kids, I wanted to eat all the time. As much as I ate at home, it was never enough, and it was never sufficiently varied to satisfy my hunger for new and unfamiliar cuisines (my mom was a very good cook, but my desire to discover new flavors was boundless.) At a young age, I began to seek out opportunities to enjoy food not typically served in my house.

On weekends, as a teenager, I would drive across my hometown of St. Louis to visit my childhood housekeeper, Mary Smith, who generously shared her Mississippi culinary traditions with me and took great pleasure in watching me devour her cooking: pan-fried chicken, collard greens, spare ribs, macaroni and cheese, sweet-potato pie. Years later, my memories of these dishes and the way they made me feel inspired me to open Blue Smoke.

On holidays—even those that my Jewish family didn't celebrate—I got to enjoy the unusual yet lovingly made creations that my grandmother served. One Christmas, she prepared steak tartare in the shape of a cow's face, canned sardines mashed up with cream cheese and Worcestershire sauce, and sautéed matzoh balls, which were served as an accompaniment to a standing rib roast. Not at all kosher, but nor was celebrating Christmas in the first place. We later adapted her recipe to become "Matzoh Polenta" at Union Square Cafe. On special occasions, there was always "Dieter's Apple Pie"—a treat made no less delicious by the fact that it was designed around my mother's calorie restrictions. As I got older, I understood that Mary Smith and my grandmother had reveled in my gustatory pleasure with every bite I took.

I was lucky to receive so much nurturing via what was on the plate, because it taught me—very early on—that cooking is an act of caring and love. The foods I enjoyed as a child, whether mouth-watering fried chicken or sugar-free, butter-free apple pie, did more than provide sustenance; they showed me that I was loved, over and over again.

When I reflected on those meals as I was preparing to open my first restaurant (Union Square Cafe, in 1985), I knew that there was this incredible, surprising pleasure to be found in feeding people. The reason I went into this business is the same reason that I continue to this day: nourishing our guests is my greatest way of expressing love.

Blue Smoke Kansas City Spareribs

Recipe by Kenny Callaghan, Executive Chef/Partner, Blue Smoke

Serves 6 to 8

2 teaspoons white sugar

1 teaspoon granulated garlic

1 teaspoon ancho chili powder

1 teaspoon chili powder

1 teaspoon ground cumin

1 teaspoon celery salt

1 teaspoon dark brown sugar

½ teaspoon Spanish paprika

½ teaspoon granulated onion

½ teaspoon ground black pepper

½ teaspoon ground white pepper

½ teaspoon kosher salt

¼ teaspoon cayenne pepper

2 full racks St.-Louis-cut spareribs (skinned)

2 cups barbecue sauce (homemade or store bought)

1. In a large bowl, mix all the spices together. Place both racks of ribs on a rimmed baking sheet. Gently massage the rub into both sides of the ribs, making sure to coat well. Cover with plastic wrap and refrigerate for 12 to 24 hours.

2. Preheat the oven to 300°F.

3. Remove the plastic wrap from the ribs and bake until very tender, about 2 hours.

4. Meanwhile, in a small saucepan, warm the barbecue sauce over low heat. Brush the warmed barbecue sauce over the tender meat and bake the ribs until the sauce glazes slightly, about 5 minutes. Remove from oven.

5. Using a sharp knife, cut ribs in between bones. For saucier ribs, apply a second coat of warmed sauce and serve. Wet naps recommended.

E.V. DAY & TED LEE

Artist / Cookbook author

Years ago, at an arts-foundation gala in an impossibly luxurious country setting, we were seated next to an astronomically famous artist who casts balloon-dogs in aluminum. He was disarmingly kind, avuncular, and inquisitive. He asked us where in New York City we lived—a subject very much on our minds. A few years earlier, we'd moved to a rental in Bedford-Stuyvesant, thinking it might take a few months for us to find a space in Brooklyn where we could live and where I could have my sculpture studio and Ted his test kitchen. We'd spent every free moment of the previous three years searching to no avail. We told him we'd come to realize we'd need a great deal of luck on our side.

"No," he said. "You already are lucky for not having found it. Stop searching—it's a *terrible* idea to live and work in the same place!"

We considered his counsel, but ultimately resolved to ignore it and are glad we did. A few years later, we found our dream space where we both can live and work. And one of the best things about it is "studio lunch"—the meal Ted makes on most days for whoever happens to be in the studio. Studio lunch has to be super-easy to prepare and serve, and it has to be flavorful, punchy, and invigorating because it's got to fortify us all for a while—we typically work late, until 7 or 8pm. Studio lunch can't be depressing or forlorn in any way.

This pork shoulder—slow-cooked with pickled jalapeños—is the kind of dish we make when I'm on a deadline and there might be five or seven assistants tromping around my studio, hanging saber-tooth tiger bones from the ceiling and silver-leafing hundreds of strands of monofilament. It's great for feeding a crowd and it's also a real crowd pleaser. It's not vegetarian by any stretch, but to date no one's ever declined it, and most tell us it's the best thing they've ever put in their mouths. We serve this recipe a lot.

Truth be told, we got the idea for this dish from our friend Mindy Merrell, who, like Ted, is a cookbook author and recipe developer, based in Nashville.

It's also true that you have to start this recipe the night before (or *very* early in the morning) if you want it ready by lunchtime. But if you've ever used a slow cooker then you know: this is truly set-it-and-forget-it cooking.

And if you've never cooked pork shoulder, there are a couple things to keep in mind when shopping. First, there are two cuts of a pig's shoulder and both work beautifully in this recipe. The upper "blade" portion of the shoulder (aka the "butt" or "Boston butt") tends to be more expensive than the lower portion of the shoulder, called the "picnic" or, in markets that cater to Hispanic consumers, the *pernil*. Picnic is cheaper than butt, principally because its bone-to-meat ratio is higher. Once the butt is cooked, you have to remove only the large blade bone, whereas with the picnic, there are several small bones to remove after cooking—no big deal.

We often serve this with wild rice or, alternatively, stuff it into tortillas with crunchy carrot or cabbage slaw, shiny with citrus and vinegar.

Slow-Cooked Pork Shoulder

Serves 8 to 10

A 6- to 9-pound bone-in pork shoulder (picnic or butt)

2 cups chicken broth or water

1 (28-ounce) can pickled jalapeños (preferably whole jalapenos with sliced carrots mixed in, but the "nacho slices" variety works too)

Kosher salt

1. Turn your slow cooker on to the "High" setting.

2. Trim skin and excess fat from the pork shoulder and place it in the slow cooker (on the rack if your cooker has one). Pour the broth and the pickled jalapeños over the shoulder. All the liquid will fall to the bottom and the jalapeños—if they're whole—will remain on top.

3. Cook until the pork is falling apart and the bones pull away with the slightest pull, 6 to 7 hours. (If you plan to be away and need a longer cooking time, turn the slow cooker to low after the first hour and cook for 8 to 9 hours more.)

4. Pull the jalapeños off the pork with tongs and reserve them to use as a garnish. Transfer the pork from the slow cooker to a large bowl or container and pull apart with a pair of forks, discarding any bones and egregiously fatty bits as you go. Strain the very delicious cooking liquid in the cooker over the pork to cover the meat (there will be 4 to 6 cups). Reserve any excess cooking liquid for another use (it makes great ramen broth!). Taste a morsel of pork with the liquid and season with salt if needed.

5. Return the pork and cooking liquid to the slow cooker and set it to "Warm" until ready to serve. (If you plan to refrigerate the pork to serve later, let the pork cool to room temperature, cover the container, and transfer to the refrigerator. Before reheating the pork, skim and discard the waxy layer of fat that will have formed on the surface.)

6. Serve the pork garnished with the reserved jalapeños.

MELISSA CLARK
Writer

This is exactly the right kind of savory, warming dish to bring to a friend who is feeling unwell. Or at least, that's why I made it in the first place.

It was for Josh, who was just back home from the hospital after being hit by a car while riding his bike. His wrist was smashed to bits and he would need a year of surgeries before he fully recovered. But, more important, his spirit was shaken. He vacillated between feelings of terror (he really could have died), anger (why was that &$%&*#! car-service driver speeding up Eighth Avenue anyway?), intense gratitude (for being alive), and deep love for his family.

Josh needed many things, and nothing, from his friends in those fragile, post-accident days, including excellent, soul-sustaining meals. That was right up my alley.

Naturally, I wanted to make him something special, but didn't know what.

So I wandered the farmers' market stalls that morning, looking for inspiration, which unveiled itself to me in the form of a small chunk of pork shoulder. Offering various shoulders to Josh and his family—to cry on and to eat—seemed appropriate for this particular dinner, and I snapped it right up.

With a pork shoulder in the bag, a cook has options. I could have roasted it surrounded by the season's last root vegetables. But by this point I was tiring of root vegetables. And a braise is always easier to transport and reheat than a roast.

For the seasonings, I wanted to simmer up something comforting but different, something vaguely exotic that would taste of a sunny, faraway place where no one ever drives SUVs at top speed down residential streets. I doubt this place

exists, but if it does, I'm sure they use plenty of dry red wine and sweet spices in their braises, along with anchovies for complexity, and tart olives and those canned plum tomatoes I had in the cupboard as a bright contrast.

I cooked it carefully and brought it over to Josh's house with some freshly made polenta and a chilled bottle of Champagne, because this dinner was a celebration—of luck, pork, dedicated bike lanes, and most important, eating good food with dear friends.

Braised Pork Shoulder with Tomatoes, Cinnamon, and Olives

From *Cook This Now!*

Serves 4 to 6

2 pounds pork shoulder (also called pork butt), cut into 2-inch chunks

Kosher salt and freshly ground black pepper

2 tablespoons olive oil

2 large leeks, halved lengthwise, rinsed well, white and light green parts sliced

5 cloves garlic, smashed and peeled

1 (28-ounce) can plum tomatoes in juice

1 cup dry red wine

5 anchovies

2-inch-length cinnamon stick

2 bay leaves

2 sprigs rosemary

⅔ cup pitted and coarsely chopped green olives

ACCOMPANIMENT

Cooked polenta

If you are making this ahead, let it cool completely and keep in the refrigerator 1 to 2 days. Remove the fat, if you like (I don't usually bother), before reheating it in the oven.

1. Preheat the oven to 300°F.

2. Pat the pork shoulder pieces dry and season generously with salt and pepper. Heat the olive oil in a 4- to 5-quart Dutch oven over medium-high heat. Sear the pork, in batches if necessary, turning occasionally, until well browned all over, about 10 minutes. Transfer the pork to a plate.

3. Add the leeks and garlic to the pot and cook, stirring, until golden, 3 to 5 minutes.

4. Return the pork to the pot and stir in the tomatoes, wine, anchovies, cinnamon stick, bay leaves, and rosemary. Cover the pot and transfer to the oven. Braise the pork, stirring once or twice, until tender, 1½ to 2 hours.

5. Raise the temperature to 425°F. Uncover the pot and stir in the olives. Continue baking, uncovered, until the liquid is reduced and the meat is very tender, about 20 minutes more. Serve over polenta.

BILL TELEPAN
Chef

Introducing new foods to your child is often a challenge, but introducing one that has a legacy in your family is downright scary. Growing up with a Hungarian mother, I have a special place in my heart for kielbasa. It was constantly present throughout my childhood. We'd grill it in the summertime, top it with sauerkraut in the winter, and, most especially, serve it at almost every holiday meal. Hundreds of pounds of kielbasa later—and enough family dinner memories to make a small feature film—one can understand my anxiety the first time I offered this sacred sausage to my daughter.

My daughter's love of beans (and my wife's hatred of sauerkraut) inspired me to make this dish. From the smoky flavor of the homemade kielbasa, which I source from a Polish butcher shop near my parents' home, to the soft texture of the white cannellini beans, I figured this would make for a solid introduction. I remember that day all too well: frantically prepping the ingredients, impatiently waiting for everything to cook, and sitting down in sheer silence with my wife and daughter to eat. After a few bites I asked my daughter what she thought, to which she replied, "Not bad!" and kept eating. I immediately texted half of my family from under the table, "Our daughter is a kielbasa fan!!!" which in my family is a giant milestone. Team Dad for the win!

Slow-Cooked Kielbasa and White Beans

Serves 4

1 pound dried cannellini beans, soaked in cold water for at least 8 hours

1 pound kielbasa

1 pound smoked ham hock or 8 ounces smoked slab bacon, cut into large pieces

2 large carrots, peeled and cut into large pieces

1 small onion, peeled and halved

4 medium cloves garlic, peeled and smashed

Kosher salt and freshly ground black pepper

1. Drain the beans and put in a slow cooker with 6 cups of cold water and the remaining ingredients. Cook on high until beans are tender, 3 to 4 hours.

2. Remove the kielbasa, the ham hock, if using, and the onion from the pot. Slice the kielbasa and remove the meat from the hock. Discard the onion. Return the meat to the pot, season with salt and pepper, and serve.

MARCUS SAMUELSSON
Chef, restaurateur

I come from the humblest of beginnings, but since my very early childhood, food has always held special meaning for me. After being adopted in Ethiopia by a Swedish family, I was raised in a loving atmosphere, surrounded by my parents, two sisters, aunts, uncles, and cousins. Some of my first memories are of cooking with my grandmother Helga. She taught me some of my favorite recipes—gravlax, roasted mackerel, preserved blueberries, potato dumplings, pickled cucumbers—but also a unique appreciation of food beyond flavor and technique. We cooked the fish that we caught and pickled or preserved the produce we gathered. We operated seasonally, not out of trendiness but out of tradition and an understanding of our surroundings. She has always remained my main inspiration in the kitchen, having instilled in me the importance of food, community, and sharing our good fortune with others.

Among the many indescribably special food experiences I've been fortunate enough to have had throughout my career and life, from playing in the legendary kitchen of el buli with Ferran Adrià to cooking the first state dinner for President Barack Obama and the prime minister of India, there is one in particular that stands out, and that is the meal served at my wedding.

When my wife, Maya, and I were married, it seemed natural for us to have the ceremony in Ethiopia. I had reconnected with my birth father and siblings who lived there, and Maya still had family and friends in her village there. She and I come from different tribes, each with its own food traditions and diet—but one ritual they have in common is that of fasting. Most days of the Ethiopian calendar are spent following a spiritual compass, which dictates diet. That means when holidays or other celebrations happen, the foods play the most significant part.

For Maya, one of the most important elements of the wedding was that her entire village—800 people—have meat to eat. That night, as we danced and sang and toasted our new life, we all shared *kitfo*—lamb tartare with fresh

cheese, collard greens, and egg. We didn't serve it because the village was without it, but because it was the only true way to celebrate.

Eating in Ethiopia is more than just preparing and presenting a meal: it's the ritual of gifting the animal, the ceremony of slaughtering the gift, and the shared experience of breaking the fast together. This feast, unlike any other, was the first time outside my grandmother's kitchen that I saw the way food creates community in more than just the figurative sense.

Warm Lamb Tartare

Serves 6

1 tablespoon berbere spice*

½ teaspoon powdered turmeric

½ teaspoon ground ginger

½ teaspoon ground cardamom

3 tablespoons olive oil

1 tablespoon unsalted butter

2 medium shallots, finely chopped

2 medium cloves garlic, finely chopped

Juice of 1 lemon

1 pound lean meat from a loin of lamb, silver skin removed, finely diced

2 teaspoons Dijon mustard

2 tablespoons thinly sliced fresh chives

1 tablespoon chopped fresh flat-leaf parsley

Kosher salt and freshly ground black pepper

1 tablespoon grated fresh peeled horseradish

1 tablespoon bleak or trout roe

ACCOMPANIMENT

Toasted pita bread

*Berbere spice can be found in Middle Eastern stores or by mail order from thespicehouse.com

1. Heat a dry skillet over medium heat until hot. Add the berbere spice, turmeric, ginger, and cardamom and toast, stirring, until fragrant, about 30 seconds. Add the olive oil, butter, shallots, garlic, and lemon juice and cook, stirring, until the garlic is golden, about 2 minutes. Remove the pan from the heat.

2. Add the lamb to the pan and toss to coat, then stir in the mustard, chives, and parsley. Season with salt and pepper.

3. With wet hands to prevent the mixture from sticking, form 6 patties, each 2 inches in diameter and ½ inch thick. Garnish with horseradish and fish roe and serve.

Editor's note: *Don't be tempted to forgo the horseradish and fish-roe garnishes; they really make the tartare sing. If you can't find a loin of lamb, buy about twice the weight in loin chops and remove bones, fat, and sinews.*

MARK SANCHEZ
Football player

I met Scotty McKnight when I was only eight years old. We became fast friends and, despite going to separate high schools and colleges, kept up a strong friendship; he is like a brother to me. His mom, Cathy, a professional chef and caterer, treats me like one of her own. Our families are very close. Whenever Scotty and I got together at his house after practice or other times, Chef Cathy always made food for us. She is an amazing cook, so it is hard to choose just one favorite dish.

This meal stands out in my memory because it marked both a major milestone in my career and a homecoming. I had just finished my second season with the Jets. We had lost to the Indianapolis Colts in the AFC Championship game, which was tough, but I was very happy and proud of how far my team went. The first meal I ate when I got home that year was Cathy's delicious filet with Gorgonzola sauce—one of my all-time favorites. All season I had been going to fancy New York City steakhouses, but nothing could beat being around the family table again, enjoying one of Cathy's delicious dinners together, and knowing that I was with the people I loved most.

Whether she is cooking me eggs for breakfast or an elaborate feast, I know how much love and passion Chef Cathy puts into every plate, and it means a great deal to me. I wish I could say I'm a pro at preparing this meal myself, but unfortunately I'm not much of a cook. Cathy is an unbelievable teacher, though, so maybe when I am done with my football career, I'll ask her to give me a few lessons!

Filet Mignon with Blue-Cheese Sauce

Serves 4

2 tablespoons unsalted butter

2 cloves garlic, minced

2 shallots, minced

½ cup red wine, preferably what you are drinking with the steak

1 tablespoon Worcestershire sauce

1. Melt the butter in a saucepan over medium heat. Add the shallot and garlic, turn the heat down to low, and cook, stirring, until softened, about 5 minutes. Add the red wine and boil until most of the wine has evaporated. Stir in the Worcestershire sauce and the cream and simmer until the sauce is reduced to about 1¼ cups. Turn the heat to low and stir in the cheese until completely melted. Remove from the heat and season with salt and pepper.

1 ½ cups heavy cream, preferably Strauss Dairy

5 ounces blue cheese, such as Rogue River Smokey Blue, Gorgonzola, or Roquefort, crumbled (1 cup)

Kosher salt and coarsely ground black pepper

4 (6- to 8-ounce) grass-fed filet mignons

1 tablespoon vegetable oil

2. While the sauce is cooking, heat a cast-iron skillet over medium-high heat. Pat the filet mignons dry and season with salt and pepper. Add the oil to the skillet and swirl the pan to coat. Cook the steaks about 4 minutes per side for medium rare (125°F to 135°F), and sear the edges briefly. Transfer the steaks to a plate, cover loosely with foil and let rest for 5 minutes.

3. Sauce the steaks generously and serve.

Editor's note: *The sauce will keep, refrigerated, for up to 3 days. Reheat gently before serving.*

DAVID BURTKA

Actor, chef

I love having my kids help out and cook with me in the kitchen, and this is a great recipe for children to participate in. When we make this dish I get out all of the spices, and we practice the difference between a cup and a tablespoon as we measure out all the ingredients. But my son's favorite part is flipping on the spice grinder and watching everything turn to dust! Another way to keep a four-year-old busy in the kitchen: have them break apart the dried porcini mushrooms.

You can prepare the cherry tomatoes a week in advance if you prefer, and keep them lying flat on a dry paper towel in an airtight container. When you roast them they will caramelize and taste sweet, like candy. It's such a great contrast to the earthy, spiced flavor of the beef.

A warning: once cooked, put these steaks under lock and key, for they have a tendency to go missing. One summer I brought six steaks inside off the grill. I left them unattended for no more than a few minutes, and when I came back there were only five steaks left and a trail of steak juice dripping off the counter and onto the floor. It didn't take me very long to find the culprit, lounging in a protein coma and licking his chops. Our dog, Watson, obviously has very refined tastes, and I'll admit—I was a little flattered.

Grilled Rib Eye Steaks with Porcini Rub, Arugula, and Oven-Dried Tomatoes

Serves 6

3 rib eyes, 1½ inches thick

½ cup dried porcini mushrooms

1 tablespoon red pepper flakes

1 tablespoon granulated garlic

4 tablespoons kosher salt

4 tablespoons black pepper

4 tablespoons white sugar

Olive oil for the grill

Bunch of arugula

½ lemon, seeds removed

Flaky sea salt, such as Maldon

Aged balsamic vinegar, for drizzling

OVEN-DRIED TOMATOES

1 pint mixed cherry tomatoes, halved

2 tablespoons olive oil

Pinch of kosher salt

Pinch of freshly ground black pepper

Pinch of dried red pepper flakes, optional

This is one of my favorite recipes. Neil and I always have some of this porcini rub on hand in case of an impromptu dinner party. It is fast, easy to make, and will really impress your friends.

1. To oven-dry the tomatoes, preheat the oven to 250°F. Put the tomatoes in a medium bowl and toss with the oil, salt, pepper, and red pepper flakes. Spread out on a rimmed baking sheet. Bake the tomatoes until semi-dried, about 3 hours. Transfer to a bowl.

2. An hour before you plan to grill the steaks, remove them from the fridge to let them come to room temperature while you prepare a hot grill fire.

3. In a small bowl, stir together the dried porcini, red pepper flakes, granulated garlic, kosher salt, pepper, and sugar. Working in batches, grind the mixture in a coffee/spice grinder to a powder.

4. Spread the porcini rub on a rimmed baking sheet. Pat the steaks dry and turn them in the rub to coat both sides evenly.

5. Brush the grill with oil and sear the steaks, 5 to 7 minutes per side, until an instant-read thermometer inserted diagonally into the center of a steak registers 125°F, for medium rare. Transfer to a rimmed baking sheet and cover loosely with foil. Let rest 10 minutes. Slice the steaks.

6. To serve, arrange arugula on a large platter, squeeze the lemon juice over it, and sprinkle with flaky salt. Arrange the steak slices on the arugula and scatter the oven-dried tomatoes over them. Drizzle with balsamic vinegar and serve.

ROBERT WILSON

Artist

In 1990 I made my first trip to Bali. During the two and a half weeks I spent there, I purchased three objects: a Timorese textile; a beautifully carved Timorese buffalo-horn spoon; and an Aitos sculpture—a tall wooden ancestral statue.

Since then, returning to Indonesia every winter, I have acquired quite an extensive collection of local artifacts. It is a country that fascinates me: the various landscapes, the social customs, the art and culture, and especially the food.

On that very first trip, 25 years ago, I visited a small restaurant that specialized in the cuisine of Timor. My favorite dish was beef rendang. Whenever I arrive in Bali, the first thing I still do is have this local dish. Through my friend Nunung, I learned to prepare it.

During the summer programs at the Watermill Center, a laboratory for the arts that I started on Eastern Long Island, we have had two Indonesian chefs. We've sometimes served more than 100 people three meals a day, in an environment that includes many objects from the different Indonesian islands. The program brings together visitors from as many as 35 nations. Beef rendang has become a specialty at the center and a favorite among the participants. It remains a unique and delicious dish, one that you don't easily find in American and Western culture. I am happy to have been able to share it with so many.

Beef Rendang

Serves 6 to 8

3 ounces tamarind pods,* skins removed

1 cup hot tap water

2 pounds boneless beef sirloin, fat trimmed

2 tablespoons coriander seeds

1 teaspoon black peppercorns

4 ounces shallots, coarsely chopped (about 1 cup)

10 small dried hot chile peppers, such as cayenne or chile de árbol

6 large cloves garlic, coarsely chopped (about 3 tablespoons)

2 tablespoons thinly sliced peeled fresh ginger

1 teaspoon ground turmeric

⅓ cup coconut oil

4 whole cloves

1 cinnamon stick

1 (13.5-ounce) can coconut milk

3 small lemongrass stalks, flattened with a meat pounder or hammer and each tied in a knot

2 tablespoons palm sugar or brown sugar

1 tablespoon kosher salt, more or less as desired

½ cup dried coconut flakes

Fresh cilantro leaves, as garnish

ACCOMPANIMENT

Cooked white basmati rice

*Tamarind pods are available in Asian and Latino markets. You can substitute ¼ cup tamarind concentrate, if that is more easily available, and dilute it with ¾ cup water.

1. Put the tamarind pods in a bowl with the hot water and let soak 1 hour.

2. Cut the beef into ½-inch-thick slices and cut slices into 2-inch lengths. Put in a large bowl.

3. In a coffee/spice grinder, grind the coriander seeds and peppercorns to a powder. Transfer to a food processor and add the shallots, peppers, garlic, ginger, turmeric, and ¼ cup of cold water. Process to a paste, pushing down the ingredients as necessary. Transfer the paste to the bowl with the meat and toss to coat.

4. Rub the tamarind pods between your fingers in the water to release all the pulp, then strain out the seeds, reserving the tamarind water (you will have about 1 cup). Set aside.

5. Heat the oil in a wok or large, heavy skillet over medium-high heat until shimmering hot. Add the cloves and cinnamon stick and cook, stirring, until the cinnamon unfurls, 1 to 2 minutes. Add the meat with the seasoning paste and cook, stirring and scraping the bottom of the pan, until the mixture is dry, about 10 minutes.

6. Add the tamarind water, coconut milk, lemongrass, sugar, and salt. Bring to a boil, then reduce the heat and simmer, stirring frequently and scraping the bottom of the pan to prevent burning, especially as the mixture gets drier, until the oil pools around the bubbles on top, and the beef is tender, 1½ to 2 hours. (If the mixture becomes very dry before the beef is tender, add a little water to continue cooking.)

7. Add half of the coconut flakes and continue to cook until the sauce is thick and dry, coating the meat.

8. Serve the rendang over rice, garnished with the remaining coconut flakes and the cilantro.

RICKY LAUREN

Author, photographer

My mother used to tell my children stories about her childhood.
During World War I, when the food supply was scarce in Vienna, her mother sent her and her sister off to spend the summers at her uncle's farm in Czechoslovakia.

There the children could have their fill of cherries, peaches, plums, and apples, which they picked straight from the trees in the orchard. And there were raspberries and strawberries, and bushes of blackberries and blueberries, which they ate to their hearts' content. They drank fresh milk and ate the cream straight from the dairy. They slathered their freshly baked, still-warm farm bread with the butter and cheese made from the milk of the cows and the goats that they tended. The chickens, ducks, and geese from the farm provided all the fresh eggs and poultry. My children and I never tired of listening to my mother as she shared those happy moments from her childhood with us.

The Austro-Hungarian Empire included Austria, Hungary, Bosnia and Herzegovina, Croatia, the Czech Republic, Slovakia, Slovenia, and parts of Italy, Montenegro, Poland, Romania, Serbia, and the Ukraine. Cultures mingled, and recipes were shared. That's how my Viennese mother ended up with a delicious Hungarian beef goulash recipe.

Hungarian Beef Goulash

Adapted from *The Hamptons* **by Ricky Lauren**

Serves 12

6 pounds beef stew meat, cut into
   1-inch chunks

Kosher salt and freshly ground
   black pepper

2 tablespoons vegetable oil, more
   as necessary

5 large onions, sliced

5 cloves garlic, chopped

1 tablespoon sweet paprika

3 cups beef stock

1 bay leaf

1 pound carrots, sliced

2 cups thawed frozen peas

3 tablespoons all-purpose flour

½ cup chopped fresh parsley

To make this an even more rustic stew, add torn pieces of crusty bread.

1. Pat the beef dry and season with salt and pepper. Heat the oil in a large pot over medium-high heat until shimmering hot. Brown the beef in batches, transferring it as it browns to a large bowl.

2. Add the onions, garlic, a little of the paprika and more oil, if necessary, to the pot and cook, stirring, until the onions are softened and reduced in volume, about 15 minutes.

3. Return the beef to the pot and sprinkle with the remaining paprika. Add 3½ cups of cold water, the beef stock, and the bay leaf and bring to a simmer. Cover, reduce the heat to low, and simmer, stirring occasionally, until the beef is almost tender, about 2 hours.

4. Add the carrots and cook until they and the beef are tender, about 30 minutes more. Add the peas and cook for 5 minutes.

5. Mix the flour with ¼ cup cold water until smooth, stir the mixture into the stew, and cook, stirring, for a few minutes, until thickened. Add the parsley, and season with salt and pepper.

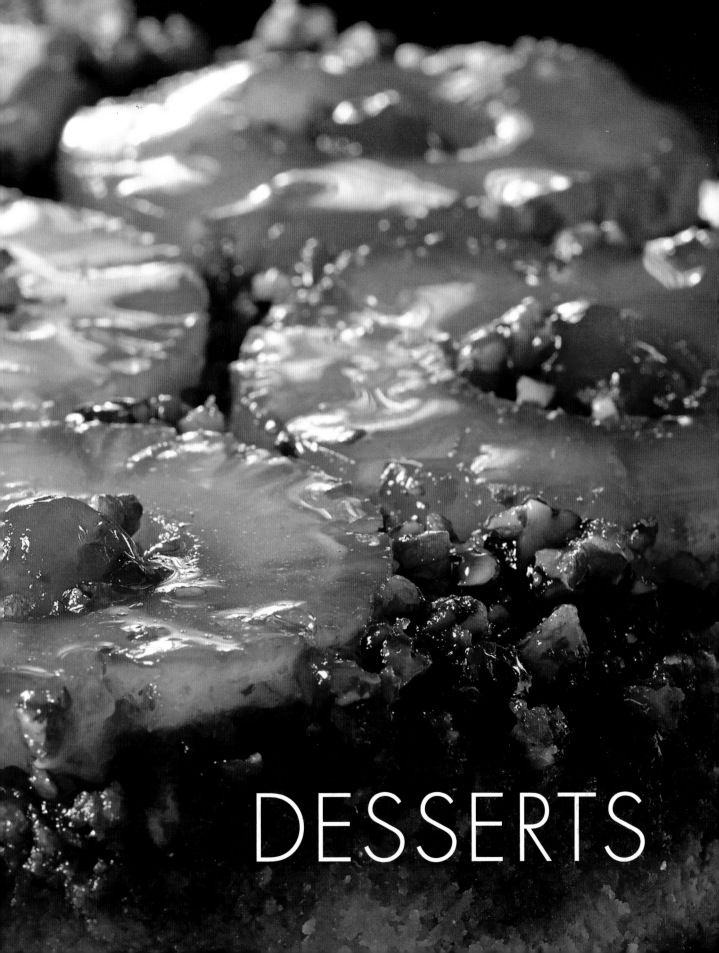

DESSERTS

DAVID VENABLE

Author, television host

There's no food that brings back fonder memories of my childhood than a beautiful peach. When I was a little boy growing up in Charlotte, North Carolina, my mother—who was a wonderful home cook and the daughter of another wonderful home cook—would take my brother, sister, and me on vacation to Georgia. It was the only time of year we really got away, because my mom was a nurse and worked full-time to support three children. But almost every single summer we headed off to Georgia and never returned home without lots of fresh, ripe summer peaches.

We usually stopped for them at a roadside stand on the way back to Charlotte, right around Gaffney, South Carolina, which is not too far from the North Carolina/South Carolina border. Gaffney is the home of a giant water tower that looks just like a peach...or a person's derriere, depending on the angle. We used to watch for that tower for hours and made a game out of who could spy it first. Whoever won got to pick which peach recipes we'd make with our bounty.

As soon as the tower was in sight, a slew of farm stands seemed to appear right in front of us. Mom would choose a lucky farmer and we would stop and squeeze every peach we could find. Then, we trekked back home to Charlotte, bushels of peaches in tow. My grandmother, who we called Burnzie, often met us there and the cooking began. We always made homemade peach ice cream, using just milk, peaches, and sugar. I still remember turning that old-fashioned crank and polishing off bowl after bowl.

Then we made peach cobbler, peach fritters, and perhaps my all-time favorite: peach praline dumplings with sweet cream. Just like an apple dumpling, peach praline

dumplings are made from whole pitted peaches. You stuff the middles with brown sugar, toasted pecans, and butter, then blanket the peaches in pastry dough. After they're baked and slightly cool, you pile a mound of homemade sweet whipped cream on top and promptly forget every care in the world. I pray you enjoy this recipe as much as we all did. And if you're ever in Gaffney, be sure to stop for a picture in front of the giant "peach."

Peach Praline Dumplings with Sweet Cream

Serves 8

1 cup pecans, toasted and finely chopped

¾ cup granulated sugar, plus 3 tablespoons

¼ cup firmly packed light brown sugar

1 ounce (2 tbs.) unsalted butter, melted

1 teaspoon vanilla extract

Cooking spray

8 ripe peaches

2 large eggs

1 (17-ounce) package frozen puff pastry sheets (2 sheets)

1 pint heavy cream

1. Put the chopped pecans, ¼ cup of the granulated sugar, and brown sugar in a medium bowl and toss to combine. Add the melted butter and vanilla and stir until combined. Set aside.

2. Line a cookie sheet with parchment paper and place a wire cooling rack on top. Lightly coat the paper and rack with cooking spray. Set aside.

3. Cut each peach in half, remove the pit, and carefully remove some of the center flesh to create a small pocket. Spoon the praline stuffing into the cavity and then pair the halves back together to form a whole peach. Set aside.

4. Whisk the eggs and 2 tablespoons of water in a small bowl to create an egg wash. Set aside.

5. On a lightly floured surface, roll each puff pastry sheet out to a 12-inch square. Cut each square into four 6-inch squares, yielding a total of eight squares.

6. Place a stuffed peach in the center of each square. Moisten the corners with a small amount of egg wash. Bring two opposite corners of the square up over the peach and press them together. Repeat with the two remaining corners. Reserve the egg wash. Place the peach dumplings on the prepared cookie sheet and freeze for 15 to 20 minutes.

7. Preheat the oven to 400°F with a rack in the lower third.

8. Remove the dumplings from the freezer. With the tines of a fork, deeply poke the bottom of each dumpling twice in a cross shape. (Be sure to insert the fork all the way through the dough and through part of the peach.) Place the dumplings back on their sheet, brush each with the remaining egg wash, and sprinkle with 3 tablespoons of the granulated sugar. Bake for 30 to 40 minutes, or until the pastry is golden brown and the peaches are fork tender.

9. Whip the heavy cream with an electric mixer until it forms soft peaks. Add the remaining ½ cup of granulated sugar and continue to whip just to stiff peaks.

10. Allow the dumplings to cool slightly before serving with the whipped cream.

SIMON DOONAN & JONATHAN ADLER

Author, fashion insider / Potter, designer, author

Our favorite recipe ever is made by our housekeeper, Larissa.
But she's so, so, so much more than a housekeeper. She's our everything. The queen of our house, the leader of our pack, the *Big Mama* to our *Cat on a Hot Tin Roof*. But most important, she makes a fab peach-and-blueberry pie. It's flawless.

On any given evening at chez nous, you can get a whiff of said pie. It's the best thing to come home to. We share a whole pie after dinner, no shame. WE KNOW: the only thing we should be thinking about when shoveling this delicious fruit delicacy into our mouths is *BACK FAT, BACK FAT, BACK FAT*. But we've got nothing but *OMG THIS IS SO GOOD* on our minds. It's the wonderful finale to any meal, or even a midnight snack, and we can never get enough of it.

We love you, Larissa.

Enjoy!

Peach-Blueberry Pie

Serves 8

PIE DOUGH

1 ¼ cups all-purpose flour

¼ teaspoon kosher salt

3 ounces (¾ stick) unsalted butter, chilled, cut into bits

1 ounce (2 tbs.) frozen vegetable shortening

3 to 4 tablespoons ice-cold water

FILLING

2 cups blueberries

6 medium-size peaches, peeled and cut into thin wedges

¼ cup sugar

2 tablespoons cornstarch

1. To make the pie dough, whisk together the flour and salt in a large bowl. Work the butter and vegetable shortening into the flour with a pastry blender or your fingers until the butter is mostly combined but still has some small, pea-sized lumps. Stir in 3 tablespoons of the water with a fork; then squeeze a small handful of the dough. If it is crumbly, stir in the remaining tablespoon of water.

2. Turn the dough out onto a work surface and form it into a mound. Smear sections of the dough outward with the palm of your hand to help incorporate the butter. Form the dough into a disk, wrap it in plastic wrap, and chill at least 1 hour.

3. To make the pie filling, set aside a handful of blueberries. Combine the remaining blueberries with the peaches, sugar, and cornstarch in a large bowl and mix well. Cover with plastic wrap and let stand for 1 hour.

4. Preheat the oven to 400°F.

5. Place the chilled pie dough on a floured work surface and with a floured rolling pin roll it out to a 12-inch round. Transfer the dough to a 9-inch pie pan. Trim and crimp the edges decoratively.

6. Line the crust with a sheet of aluminum foil and fill with dried beans or rice. Blind bake the crust until the edges are firm and pale golden, about 15 minutes. Remove the foil and beans and continue to bake until a pale golden color, about 10 minutes.

7. Stir the filling and pour it into the crust. If desired, arrange the peach wedges around the edge to resemble a flower; place the reserved blueberries in the center. Bake until bubbling all over, 30 to 45 minutes. Let cool slightly on a rack before serving.

MEREDITH VIEIRA

Journalist, talk show and game show host

I never needed a calendar to know when it was Thanksgiving. The day before, my mom would always bake her homemade apple pies. First, we would flour a portion of the kitchen table. Then, out came the box of Jiffy piecrust mix. I would sit there mesmerized by her slender, beautifully manicured fingers as they formed two balls of dough. Onto the flour they would plop, and each of us would grab a rolling pin. Her crust never stuck to the pin. Mine always did. She would hold my sticky fingers in hers and we would laugh hysterically.

I realize now how patient my mom was. She could have done the job in half the time without my "help." Did I mention the extra apples she had to slice because one little girl couldn't resist putting the juicy morsels in her mouth instead of in the pie?

While the pies were cooking, we would sit on the linoleum floor and play jacks until the timer went off. Then Mom would open the kitchen window and let the November air cool down our masterpieces.

The next evening we would gather around the dining-room table with our extended family. Just as giving thanks transitioned into heated political debate (which it always did!), the smell of warm apple pie would envelop us all. I devoured every flaky piece before the plates could be cleared.

I didn't grow up to be a good cook, except when it comes to apple pie. Every Thanksgiving, I try to recreate Elsie's recipe. The paper it's written on has turned yellow with time. And some of the instructions are smudged, the result of spilled water, or perhaps wine. Unlike my mom's fingers, mine are short, my nails bitten. I long ago surrendered the Jiffy and now purchase Pillsbury's ready-made piecrusts. So maybe all the ingredients aren't quite the same, except for the most important one: love.

Elsie's Apple Pie

Makes one 9-inch pie

PIECRUST

2½ cups all-purpose flour

½ teaspoon kosher salt

6 ounces (1½ sticks) unsalted butter, chilled, cut into bits

1. Whisk together the flour and salt in a large bowl. Work the butter and vegetable shortening into the flour with a pastry blender or your fingers until the butter is mostly combined but still has some small, pea-sized lumps. Stir in 5 tablespoons of the water with a fork, then squeeze a small handful of the dough. If it is crumbly, stir in the remaining tablespoon of water.

2 ounces (¼ cup) frozen vegetable shortening

5 to 6 tablespoons ice-cold water

FILLING

6 medium apples, preferably a mix of Macintosh and Granny Smith, peeled, cored, and sliced

1 egg white, lightly beaten

½ cup sugar

1 teaspoon apple-pie spice

1 tablespoon unsalted butter, cut into 4 pieces

1 tablespoon milk

2. Turn the dough out onto a work surface and form into a mound. Smear sections of the dough outward with the palm of your hand to help incorporate the butter. Form the dough into two disks, one slightly larger than the other, wrap them in plastic wrap, and chill at least 1 hour.

3. Preheat the oven to 425°F.

4. Roll out the larger disk of dough on a floured work surface with a floured rolling pin to a 12-inch round. Transfer the dough to a 9-inch pie pan. Brush with some of the beaten egg white. Mound the apple slices in the crust.

5. Mix the sugar and apple-pie spice in a small bowl and sprinkle over the apples. Dot the apples with the butter.

6. Roll out the smaller disk of dough in the same manner to an 11-inch round. Cut four (2-inch) slits in the dough to let the steam escape and lay the dough over the apples. Press the edges of the two crusts together, cut off the excess, fold the edges under themselves, and crimp decoratively.

7. Mix the remaining egg white with the milk and brush over the top crust. Bake on a rimmed baking sheet until the crust is golden brown and the apples are tender, 40 to 45 minutes.

8. Let cool before serving.

ALEX GUARNASCHELLI

Chef

There is nothing like experiencing true hunger and finding that bite of food that feeds you in every way.

A few years ago, my mother was hospitalized and underwent an operation that lasted a number of hours. I don't remember breathing much while she was in surgery. Afterward, I just waited for her to open her eyes and look on me as she had thousands of times in my life. All I wanted was that look to know she was back.

I sat by her bed as she slept. She was breathing uncomfortably. I didn't care: she was breathing. That's almost all I needed. Her eyes opened slightly and she squinted and adjusted to the light and her surroundings. "I feel so

hungry," she whispered through parched lips. I fumbled around in my bag for something, anything to give her and found I had a Braeburn apple from the Union Square greenmarket. I knew it was a good, juicy apple. Tart. Tangy.

Why did I have an apple in my bag? I love Michael Pollan's "Rule #4: If you're not hungry enough to eat an apple, then you're probably not hungry." Carrying around an apple seemed a realistic way to measure my own hunger. And now I was going to put that method to the test with my mother. She was never much of an apple eater beyond pies, but she took the apple and bit through the

skin. I watched as she almost sucked the juice from the apple with that first bite and then chewed and swallowed. "This is the best apple I have ever had in my life. What is it?" She looked at me. "A Braeburn from the market," I answered.

I was moved beyond words. She needed me as much as I needed her. And she also needed to share that apple with me. The power of a simple raw ingredient at the right moment, when we are truly hungry for it, is profound.

Feeding other people. Watching them become whole again through the restorative power of food and love. That's what it's all about.

Apple Crisp

Serves 6 to 8

3 pounds Granny Smith apples (about 8)

1 cup light brown sugar

1 tablespoon unsulfured molasses

Finely grated zest and juice of 1 lemon

Finely grated zest and juice of 1 navel orange

½ teaspoon ground cinnamon

½ teaspoon ground dried ginger

⅛ teaspoon ground nutmeg

¾ teaspoon kosher salt

1½ cups all-purpose flour

4 ounces (1 stick) lightly salted butter, chilled and cut into cubes, plus 1 tablespoon for greasing the baking dish

I would love to take full credit for this recipe but it is simply the recipe my mother made year after year when I was growing up. So simple and delicious. I love all apples but my newest favorites are Braeburn and Rome varieties. For this recipe, however, I use pure Granny Smith: tart, tried, and true.

1. Preheat the oven to 375°F.

2. Core and peel the apples. Cut them in half lengthwise and then crosswise into ¼-inch slices. Place the slices in a large bowl with ⅓ cup of the brown sugar, the molasses, lemon and orange zest and juice, cinnamon, ginger, nutmeg, and ½ teaspoon of the salt. Toss to blend.

3. In a large bowl, combine the flour, the remaining ⅔ cup of brown sugar, and the remaining ¼ teaspoon salt. Add the cubed butter and work it into the dry ingredients until it forms large crumbs.

4. Grease the bottom and sides of a 9 by 13-inch baking dish with a tablespoon of butter. Layer the apple slices in the dish and cover evenly with the topping mixture.

5. Place the dish in the center of the oven and bake until the apple slices are tender when pierced with the tip of a knife and the topping is golden brown, about 45 minutes. Let cool a few minutes before serving.

KATIE WORKMAN
Cookbook author

Before my dad died, he was sick for six months. A long time. No, a short time. Kind of a lifetime. It was brain cancer, and the kind where from the beginning you know what the end of the story will be, you just don't know how many pages the book has or what happens in the chapters leading up to the end.

My dad was an amazing man. I can say it, and mean it, but he was the kind of amazing man where a lot of other people say it too.

Dad was an eater. Boy, did he love food. And like all great eaters, he was just as eye-rolling happy with a fantastic tuna salad and a box of Triscuits as he was with a multi-course meal at Le Bernardin. He was probably happiest if there were ribs involved. We are a full-on food family; my mother, my sister, and I all cook, we entertain, we are the type of family that talks about lunch with our mouths full of breakfast.

Dad talked about really good food the same way he talked about a stirring symphony or a wonderful piece of art: with reverence and huge joy. There were italics in the way he spoke of something he loved. "That cheese is *marvelous*!" She made a chocolate tart that was, in fact, very possibly *the best chocolate tart in the world*." "The meal was just simply *extraordinary*. No really, it was *extraordinary*." He really wanted you to understand Just. How. Good. This. Was. Though often from the look on his face you couldn't quite know how extraordinary the meal had been.

He ate very slowly. Like, very slowly. As in, on any typical Thanksgiving people were starting on the pies and he was reaching for another wing.

It took a little while for his appetite to change and there were ebbs and flows. Early on there were still requests for pastrami sandwiches, turkey with all the trimmings. At the end a sip of apple juice was a chore.

Right after his surgery in late September, which was right after his diagnosis, he was in the hospital and a specialist came in and cheerfully announced, "Hi,

I'm Cindy from Swallowing!" It wasn't a joke: she was there to evaluate his ability to chew and swallow. She spooned a little canned pear into his mouth, and then let him nibble a Lorna Doone. "I think we can put you onto a mechanical diet!" she announced, explaining that that meant small bits of pre-cut soft foods. She left. Dad looked at me, opened a bag of pretzels someone had left lying around, and ate them. Bite that, Cindy from Swallowing.

We all made food for him. Sometimes he wanted to eat it, sometimes he didn't. Sometimes he would take a bite, sometimes he would eat a real meal, sometimes he would just smile and shrug.

The night before Christmas, he was back in the hospital. I told him I would bring dinner the next night, and asked him what he wanted. He didn't know. I suggested chicken soup, noodle pudding—unchallenging, gentle foods. "How about prime rib?" suggested a visiting friend. "Oh yes, and Yorkshire pudding!" he said. And the next night he ate it, our family sitting in a shitty windowless conference/supply room with hideous fluorescent lights and the occasional nurse popping into the room to grab a fresh bandage or catheter for another patient.

Toward the end, when he wasn't eating much at all, I cut a paper-thin sliver of pear and handed it to him. He ate it very slowly. His nurse and I looked at each other with raised eyebrows, a silent tiny triumph. I handed him another transparent slice. Then another. One hour later, the pear was eaten. It was the most beautiful core of fruit I have ever seen.

Roasted Pears and Custard

Serves 2 to 4

2 firm-ripe Bartlett pears

¼ cup granulated sugar

½ teaspoon vanilla extract

2 large egg yolks

1 cup heavy cream

This is a recipe from my dear friend Christopher Idone. It has much meaning, as not only does it feature pears, which clearly make me think of my dad, but it of course also makes me think of Christopher. I was one of a small handful of Christopher's closest friends who cared for him during his last months. He was one of the creators of the book you have in your hands right now, and he was an immensely skilled cook and a magnetic person. I loved him a lot.

1. Preheat the oven to 400°F.

2. Peel the pears and halve lengthwise, trying to split the stems as well. Core with a melon baller to create a well in each half, and cut slivers off the round bottoms so they will sit easily. Arrange the pears, cut side up, in a small, shallow baking dish. Divide the sugar among the core wells and sprinkle with the vanilla.

3. Bake the pears in the middle of the oven until the sugar is caramelized and the edges of the pears are browned, 15 to 20 minutes.

4. Meanwhile, whisk together the egg yolks and cream in a small bowl.

5. Pour the cream mixture around (not over) the pears and return the baking dish to the oven. Turn off the heat and leave in the oven until the custard is set, 15 to 20 minutes.

MICHAEL KORS
Fashion designer

I had the ultimate Jewish grandmother. But she was a high-school principal and also very scientific. She loved fashion, she loved style, and she loved baking, I think because it was like alchemy. Particularly something like her pineapple upside-down cake. First, it has all these dry ingredients that transform into something totally different. Then there's the thrill of flipping the pan perfectly when you take it out of the oven, and finding that glaze at the bottom of the cake. I think she looked at it like a food science project.

What's funny about it, too, is that I made it once on Martha Stewart's show, and when I got there Martha looked at me and said, "Canned pineapple and canned maraschino cherries for garnish? No, no, Michael, no, it has to be fresh." And I said, "No, no. This recipe is from the era when there was something magical about the fact that fruit could be canned. In fact, I tried it once with fresh pineapple and it didn't work. And you need all that red food dye in the maraschino cherries because it turns into a little party on the plate."

A funny coincidence is that Bette Midler worked at the Dole pineapple plant when she was a kid growing up in Honolulu. So I like to imagine that somehow, at some point, my grandmother made a pineapple upside-down cake with a can of Dole pineapple that Bette Midler packed. Wouldn't that be the best?

Grandma Bea's Pineapple Upside-Down Cake

Makes one (9-inch) round cake

1 (20.5 ounce) can pineapple rings with juice

6 ounces (1½ sticks) unsalted butter, softened

1 cup light brown sugar

1 small jar maraschino cherries

1 cup chopped pecans

4 large eggs

A cast-iron skillet is ideal for preparing this cake and helps it caramelize while baking.

1. Preheat the oven to 325°F.

2. Drain the pineapple rings. Place the pineapple rings on a wire rack and continue to drain.

3. In a 9-inch cast-iron skillet or round cake pan (not spring form), melt 2 ounces (½ stick) of the butter over medium heat. Stir in the brown sugar until evenly moistened and remove the pan from the heat. Place 1 whole

2 large egg yolks

1½ teaspoon vanilla extract

1½ cups all-purpose flour

1 teaspoon baking powder

½ teaspoon table salt

1½ cups granulated sugar

slice of pineapple in the center of the pan and surround with 7 more slices. Place cherries in the centers of the pineapple slices. Firmly press the pecans into the gaps between the slices.

4. In a bowl, whisk the eggs and egg yolks with the vanilla until smooth and lemony in color.

5. In the bowl of an electric mixer, combine the dry ingredients and mix at low speed. Add the remaining butter and mix at low speed until blended. Using a rubber spatula, scrape down the sides. Gradually add the egg mixture in small batches and beat at medium speed until the eggs are incorporated and the batter is smooth. Scrape the batter into the fruit-lined pan, smoothing evenly with the spatula.

6. Bake in the middle of the oven until golden brown and a cake tester inserted in the center comes out clean, 1 to 1¼ hours. Place the pan on a wire rack and cool for 10 minutes.

7. Run a small sharp knife around the edge of the pan to release the cake. Place a large serving plate over the pan and invert onto the plate. Any fruit that sticks to the pan can easily be removed with a small metal spatula and returned to the top of the cake. Serve.

BLAINE TRUMP

Fundraiser

It's been quite a journey. I joined God's Love We Deliver way back in 1986 when the AIDS pandemic hit New York and people were being sent home from the hospital to basically die without any support. There were no cocktails to take then. We'd deliver a meal to someone on Monday and not be sure they would still be there Tuesday. It was a very scary time.

I remember receiving a letter from the organization one afternoon which said, "This is what we're doing, and we're reaching out to you for support because we need help, we need volunteers, we need funding, and we're in the basement of this church over on the west side." I'll never forget it. I literally put the letter down, took a taxi straight over there, and knocked on the door. And we just sat down and talked. The need was so clear. I had several friends suffering with AIDS, so what they were doing touched me to the core. I said, "I'm going to give up everything else and help you guys."

In the beginning, I delivered quite a bit. And it was very difficult, because we were losing so many people. And then things started to turn, and I felt my strengths were best used to raise money. But I've always enjoyed the deliveries the most. It is so gratifying to go into someone's home, to bring them a good meal and make them laugh. You can't help but feel that you're doing something truly important. You're a lifeline. It is a beautiful thing to be able to give someone happiness, hope, and nutrition.

I grew up in a family where food was love. My parents are both from the South and they adored great food. My mother, particularly, was a wonderful cook, and the influence of Southern cuisine was always in her kitchen. She taught me that dinner is a special time to get together and talk about what's going on in the world. So I have a rule now: no cell phones, no iPads at the table. It's a time to sit down, share a delicious meal, and catch up with family and friends.

When I was young, Mother used to make carrot cake all the time, and I

loved it. The recipe came from my godmother. And then, when I had my son, I always made it for his birthday. I'd do two round layers side by side to make a clown. To this day, it's probably his favorite cake. One day I hope he will share it with his own kids.

Carrot Cake

Serves 12

CAKE

Butter for greasing the pans

2 cups all-purpose flour

2 cups sugar

2 teaspoons baking powder

2 teaspoons baking soda

1 teaspoon mace

1 teaspoon ground cinnamon

1 teaspoon ground nutmeg

1 teaspoon fine salt

1 cup vegetable oil

4 large eggs, lightly beaten

3 cups grated carrots (from
   1 pound carrots)

ICING

3 (8-ounce) packages Philadelphia
   cream cheese

4 ounces (1 stick) unsalted butter,
   softened

1 cup confectioners' sugar

1 teaspoon vanilla extract

1 cup finely chopped pistachios

1. Preheat the oven to 350°F. (If your oven isn't big enough to fit all 3 baking pans on the middle rack, put the oven racks in the upper and lower thirds of the oven and switch the cake pans halfway through baking.)

2. Butter the bottoms and sides of three 8-inch cake pans. Cut out three 8-inch rounds of parchment, line bottoms of pans, and butter the parchment.

3. In a large bowl, whisk together the dry ingredients. Add the oil, eggs, and carrots and whisk to combine well. Divide the batter among the cake pans (the batter will be very shallow).

4. Bake the cakes until a wooden pick comes out clean, 28 to 32 minutes. Transfer to a rack to cool for 10 minutes, turn the cakes out of the pans, and let cool completely.

5. To make the icing, combine the cream cheese, butter, confectioners' sugar, and vanilla in a large bowl. Beat, using an electric mixer, until smooth and fluffy.

6. Put 1 of the cake layers on a cake plate (protect the cake with 3 strips of parchment placed partially under the edges of the cake). Ice and stack each of the 3 cake layers and then ice the sides of the cake. Decorate the sides with the pistachios. Remove the parchment strips and serve.

Editor's note: *The iced cake can stand at room temperature for up to 3 hours. It can be made a day ahead and refrigerated, loosely covered. Let come to room temperature before serving.*

ROSANNE CASH

Singer-songwriter, author

Mario Batali once asked me to describe my perfect meal. It was hard for me to decide on an entree, a side dish, the kind of wine, and the location, but there was no question about the dessert. It had to be coconut cake. I was also asked what I wanted at my funeral (a morbid notion, but strangely delightful to consider) and my first thought was that I wanted people to eat coconut cake in my memory.

Why coconut cake? It connects me to a lot of women in my family and reminds me of joyful occasions and the best of times. My mother, Vivian,

Kristen DeLauer and Rosanne's daughter Carrie Crowell.

and her mother, Irene, made "Four-Layer Dessert," which included a healthy amount of coconut. Perhaps that's where the obsession began. My paternal grandmother, Carrie, also made the most unbelievable coconut pie, a quintessential Southern dessert that nearly put you in a coma with its delirious amount of sugar. It was more drug than dessert. I got excited every time I saw that pie.

One of my dearest and oldest friends, Kristen DeLauer, invented the most badass recipe for coconut cake you have ever tasted, and my daughter Carrie has improvised on that recipe to put the family stamp on it—just as badass and completely delicious. It's become such a part of our tradition that it's not really my birthday unless there is coconut cake.

I imagine in future generations there will be more riffs on our shared recipe, but let this serve as official notice to my descendants: coconut cake is a family institution and the recipe an heirloom, and I expect that they will preserve the tradition, make the cake, and serve it at important celebrations (and sometimes just because it is Monday and the week will go better with a little coconut cake to grease the wheels).

It's strange, the things you feel passionate about. Sometimes there is no rhyme or reason, but the passion still has to be honored. Don't forget to eat it at my funeral.

Coconut Cake

Recipe by Rosanne Cash, Kristen DeLauer, and Carrie Crowell

Makes one 9-inch layer cake

CAKE

6 ounces (1½ sticks) unsalted butter, softened, more for greasing the pans

3 cups plus 3 tablespoons all-purpose flour

4½ teaspoons baking powder

1½ teaspoons salt

2 cups granulated sugar

1½ teaspoons coconut extract/flavoring

3 large eggs

1½ cups whole milk

½ cup canned (crushed or diced) pineapple, drained

FILLING AND FROSTING

2 cups granulated sugar

16 ounces full-fat sour cream

21 ounces flaked or shredded coconut (sweetened or the unsweetened, according to preference)

1½ cups heavy cream

1. Preheat the oven to 350°F. Butter and flour two 9-inch round cake pans (preferably 2 inches deep, with straight, not tapered, edges).

2. In a medium bowl, sift together the flour, baking powder, and salt.

3. In a large bowl, using a wooden spoon or electric mixer, cream the butter, sugar, and coconut extract until light and fluffy. Add the eggs one at a time, mixing after each. Alternately add the flour mixture (in 3 batches), and the milk (in 2 batches), mixing after each addition. Mix in the pineapple and beat until combined. Pour the batter into the prepared pans, spreading evenly.

4. Bake until the cakes start to pull away from the sides of the pans and a cake tester comes out clean, 30 to 35 minutes. Transfer the pans to racks to cool 10 minutes, then turn the cakes out onto the racks to cool completely.

5. To make the filling, stir together the sugar, sour cream, and 14 ounces of the coconut in a large bowl. Remove and reserve 1 cup of this filling mixture.

6. To assemble, using a bread knife, split each cake in two horizontally. Put one layer of the cake cut side up on a cake plate (protect the plate by putting 3 strips of parchment paper partially under the cake) and spread with a third of the filling. Repeat with 2 more layers and top with the last layer, cut side down.

7. To make the frosting, beat the heavy cream in a large bowl using a whisk or electric mixer until medium peaks form. Fold in the reserved sour-cream filling. Frost the top and sides of the cake.

8. Cover the cake and refrigerate for up to 1 day before serving. Up to 2 hours before serving, press the remaining 7 ounces of coconut onto the top and sides of the cake.

SANDRA LEE

Television personality, author, magazine editor

If you were to ask anyone in my family, they would tell you my favorite thing to do is *eat*. Then they would tell you I'm usually already planning my next meal before I've even finished the one in front of me. It's all true. I love to eat, I love to cook, and I love to bake.

My earliest memories of cooking were with my Grandma Lorraine. She loved being in the kitchen. To her it was the center of our home and a place to be enjoyed. I fondly remember baking with Grandma in her cottage on Grant Street, which was just a few blocks from the Pacific Ocean. She made the most fantastic cakes. Her buttercream frosting and vanilla cake was my favorite. My birthday and my sister Cindy's are only four days apart, and every year Grandma baked each of us our own special cake.

With a flip of her wrist, she turned two ordinary disposable aluminum pie pans into grand, shiny silver cake pedestals. On top of each, she placed a single 8-inch cake, which she iced with white frosting, giving her a perfect canvas for dozens of bright pink flowers.

I learned from her how to serve delicious and beautiful meals and desserts without the hassle and stress. She taught me that being a great gourmet is not a requirement for the enjoyment of eating or cooking food, and that being a good cook—even a great cook—is easy.

Grandma Lorraine's Birthday Cake

Makes 2 (8-inch) cakes

1 (15.25-ounce) box yellow cake mix

3 eggs

⅓ cup vegetable oil

1 cup white cranberry juice

2½ teaspoons raspberry extract

1 (16-ounce) can white frosting

1. Preheat the oven to 325°F. Grease the bottoms and sides of two 8-inch round dark or nonstick cake pans.

2. In a large bowl, combine the cake mix, eggs, vegetable oil, white cranberry juice, and 1½ teaspoons of the raspberry extract with an electric mixer on medium speed, or beat by hand for 2 minutes. Pour batter into pans.

3. Bake for approximately 30 minutes or until a toothpick comes out clean.

4 (6-ounce) tubes pink writing
    icings, Wilton

Flower and letter candy
    decorations, Wilton

Candy rainbow sprinkles, Wilton

4. Remove cakes from the oven and let cool in the pans for 10 minutes.
Remove cakes from their pans and transfer to racks to cool completely.

5. Place each cake on top of an inverted 9-inch aluminum pie pan.

6. Add the remaining teaspoon of raspberry extract to the white frosting
and stir to combine thoroughly.

7. Frost the top and sides of each cake. Use a pastry bag with a star tip
to pipe pink icing around the bottom of each cake where it meets the pie
pan. Decorate as desired.

BILL YOSSES
Pastry chef

We were asked to join a meeting in the "Map Room," a room with historical gravitas like few others. FDR had worked on his World War II strategy there and the military maps were still on the wall. It was the new administration's first few weeks in the White House and the meeting was called in this always-locked, "off limits" room, which is not open to visitors or staff—so there was considerable suspense: Who was getting fired?

No one, it turned out. In fact, we were being asked to participate in a new initiative spearheaded by the First Lady, and to assist in its implementation.

The program, which came to be known as "Let's Move," did not even have a name at that point, but it was obvious that it was going to be very important. I began to think of how many challenges Mrs. Obama had to face at that time in her life: moving her family from Chicago to DC, transferring the kids to a new school, learning about this strange new place: a home, a museum, and a fortress. Yet she took the time out in those hectic first days to talk to her kitchen staff about the importance of childhood and adult nutrition, and about her determination, through the influential office of the First Lady, to combat the obesity and diabetes epidemic we were facing as a country. Her delegate in this effort was Sam Kass, who had cooked for the Obamas in Chicago and had started sustainability and food awareness groups there.

So we chefs began to meet with Sam to understand the types of foods our new boss liked, and to assist him in planting a garden on the South Lawn of the White House. There had been gardens before, but this was on a new scale. Eleanor Roosevelt had grown a small victory garden, and there was actually an entire orangery built by President Andrew Jackson that stood on the spot where the West Wing is now. His famous magnolia trees still rise up proudly on either side of the south portico and bear giant flowers every year.

There is a huge bureaucratic system in Washington, DC (surprised?), and it took a lot of work for Sam to get the garden started but he succeeded, and a beautiful plot was planted in March 2009. Very few chefs have the opportunity to walk out their back door and pick their produce right from the ground (and year-round, no less, thanks to the hoop houses). It was a privileged position to be in, no question, but it was hard work, too. Weeding during the dead of summer in the White House's backyard is no different from weeding in 100-degree heat anywhere else. Yet tending that garden and experiencing the wide range of flavors that it produced was a great blessing.

It was not only a source of sustenance but of inspiration as well, and we brought school kids in twice a week to visit the garden and learn about where food comes from. The marvelous botanist Steve Jones from Washington State University advised us on what grains to plant, and though the amounts were too small to actually mill into flour, it gave me amazing insight into the nutritional benefits and flavors of wheat and other grains.

We never compromised on the quality of our desserts in the pastry kitchen, but we incorporated ingredients from the garden and a healthier pantry to expand flavor profiles and add nutrients instead of empty calories. By using a wider variety of grains, for example, we enhanced the nutty, earthy, umami flavors of our confections.

Of all the recipes that developed from that experience I am thrilled to share one of my very favorites.

Matcha Green Tea Whole-Grain Pound Cake

Makes 1 (8-inch) loaf

Butter to grease the pan

1 cup all-purpose flour, more
to flour the pan

½ cup sugar

Finely grated zest of 2 limes

½ cup buttermilk

¼ cup fresh lime juice

3 large eggs

¼ teaspoon vanilla extract

¾ cup whole-grain flour

1 tablespoon matcha (Japanese
powdered green tea)

1½ teaspoons baking powder

¼ teaspoon baking soda

¼ teaspoon fine salt

⅔ cup mild extra-virgin olive oil

GLAZE

2 tablespoons powdered sugar

2 tablespoons fresh lime juice

1. Preheat the oven to 350°F. Butter and flour an 8-inch loaf pan.

2. Combine the sugar and lime zest in a large bowl and rub together with your fingers until it feels like wet sand. Whisk in the buttermilk, lime juice, eggs, and vanilla.

3. Whisk together the all-purpose and whole-grain flours, matcha, baking powder, baking soda, and salt in another bowl. Whisk the dry ingredients into the batter, and then whisk in the oil.

4. Pour the batter into the prepared pan. Bake until a tester inserted into the center comes out clean, about 55 minutes (edges may be brown). Be careful not to overbake.

5. Transfer the pan to a rack to cool slightly, then turn the cake out onto the rack and turn right side up.

6. To make the glaze, whisk together the powdered sugar and lime juice. Brush the glaze over the top and sides of the warm cake. Let cool completely before slicing.

KATIE COURIC

Journalist, author, news anchor, TV personality

My mom wasn't the best cook but she was the best mom.
She had four kids to raise and her repertoire was pretty basic and fairly typical
of American fare in the 1960s and '70s. Meatloaf with Campbell's tomato
soup poured on the top, pot roast surrounded by potatoes and carrots, baked
cut-up chicken lying languidly in a pool of melted butter, just waiting to be
sopped up by a piece of white bread. She went on a turkey Tetrazzini jag
once—a somewhat exotic departure—when I was in junior high school. She
made a mean potato salad in the summer and I still prepare her pear and lime
Jell-O concoction (with a ball of cream cheese and pecans stuffed in the pear)
every Thanksgiving.

But the dish that makes me think of my mom and her mother, who we
called Nana (pronounced NAH-na), the most, are the brownies she made on a
semi-regular basis. They are, quite simply, the best brownies on the planet: the

kind you whip up from a box just can't compete. We baked them together countless times. Spooned into a square tin pan (minus the batter I had consumed from the spoon and bowl—my mom never used a mixer, just old-fashioned "elbow grease") they came out of the oven, moist and dense, often with the ubiquitous pecans present in the pantries of transplanted Southerners everywhere. The shiny surface was dusted with confectioners' sugar straight from our flour sifter, slightly discolored by age. And there they were, sitting in that square pan, cooling on the stove, their chocolate perfume filling the kitchen in our house in Arlington, Virginia, just waiting for us to cut into their still slightly warm deliciousness.

My mom died on Labor Day, which, given her industrious nature and childbearing prowess, seemed fitting. I think of her every day and miss her terribly. My siblings and I divided up her possessions; I am lucky to have a number of beautiful things—some, like the little wooden man who held toothpicks in his mouth on the kitchen windowsill, are purely sentimental. And who knew that a lamp, rarely noticed for years, could now evoke such joy, sadness, and longing, and make Mom's hands, her infectious laugh, and her fierce and unconditional love come alive again?

But one of my most prized possessions is her metal recipe box, full of index cards with the neat, block letters that characterized her handwriting. The first card bears her brownie recipe. It's not fancy or complicated, but it's full of love, and most important, memories of a mother I am forever grateful to have called mine.

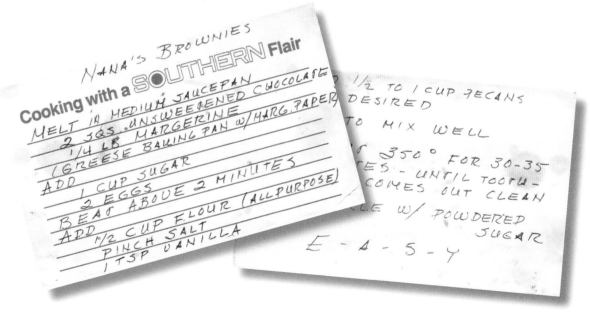

271

Brownies

Makes 16 (2-inch) brownies

4 ounces (1 stick) unsalted butter or margarine, more for greasing the pan

½ cup all-purpose flour, more for coating the pan

2 (1-ounce) squares unsweetened chocolate

1 cup granulated sugar

2 large eggs

Pinch of salt

1 teaspoon vanilla extract

½ to 1 cup chopped pecans, optional

Confectioners' sugar

1. Preheat the oven to 350°F.

2. Grease an 8 by 8-inch baking pan with butter or margarine. Sprinkle a little flour in the pan to coat bottom and sides. Knock out excess.

3. Put the butter or margarine in a saucepan with the chocolate and melt gently over low heat, stirring occasionally. Remove from heat, add sugar and eggs, and beat with a handheld electric mixer on medium speed for 2 minutes. Add the flour, salt, vanilla, and pecans and stir to combine.

4. Transfer the batter to the baking pan and bake until a toothpick comes out with a few crumbs adhering, 30 to 35 minutes. Place the pan on a rack to cool.

5. Dust the cooled brownies with confectioners' sugar and cut into 16 squares. Serve.

ISABELLA ROSSELLINI

Actor

My mother, Ingrid Bergman, used to say that her favorite word was "room service." I don't remember my mother ever cooking, although she loved cleaning. She taught me how to efficiently and thoroughly wash dishes, glasses, pots, and pans after our meals. I still excel at it and seldom ever use a dishwasher.

Once, Momma, wanting to be "normal" for us kids, decided to do what, generally, other mothers do: bake cookies.

Since she was Swedish, she settled on the typical ginger snaps, called *pepparkaka*.

When Momma's *pepparkaka* came out of our oven, they didn't have the rusty color of the ones we bought at the supermarket; they were much darker. They smelled good, but when we tried to eat the cookies, we couldn't bite into them. They were too hard. They looked and felt like some sort of Paleolithic cookies.

Disappointed, we decided to make the best of it and went to a nearby beach to make a feast for the seagulls, who are known to eat everything. The seagulls, though, had the same problem we did. They couldn't bite through the cookies.

Then I saw a clever bird fly up high with one of Momma's *pepparkaka* in its beak and drop it to smash it on the rocks—the same technique they use to open oysters.

Unlike the oysters, Momma's cookie remained intact!

Pepparkaka Cookies

Makes about 4 dozen 2- to 3-inch cookies

8 ounces (2 sticks) unsalted butter

1 large egg

1 cup granulated sugar

1 tablespoon pure maple syrup

½ teaspoon baking soda

2 teaspoons ground cardamom

1 teaspoon ground cinnamon

½ teaspoon ground ginger

½ teaspoon ground cloves

2½ cups all-purpose flour

1. Melt the butter in a small saucepan and let cool.

2. In a large bowl, beat the egg, sugar, syrup, baking soda and spices. Stir in the melted butter. Stir in the flour to make a dough. Gather it into a ball, wrap in plastic wrap, and refrigerate for 24 hours.

3. Preheat the oven to 375°F. Place a rack in the middle of the oven.

4. Roll the dough out to a ⅛-inch-thick round. Cut out cookies in decorative shapes and arrange about 1 inch apart on parchment-lined baking sheets. Bake each sheet until cookies are lightly browned, 8 to 10 minutes. Transfer to racks to cool. Store in an airtight container for up to 2 weeks.

LAUREN BUSH LAUREN

Social entrepreneur, philanthropist

One of my coziest childhood memories is of homework hour with my siblings after school.
On special days, if we had a particularly big test or project coming up, my mom would pop some amazing chocolate chip cookies into the oven. I loved the smell of the dough rising as they baked, knowing that she took the time
to make them for us (even if they were occasionally the "slice-and-bake" kind). They were her special way of saying she was there for us and proud of us. The smell of chocolate chip cookies baking still takes me back to those
afternoons with flashcards strewn around the kitchen table.

Probably because of this, in my adult life I constantly
crave chocolate chip cookies. I'm the first to admit that baking
isn't really my strong suit, but I've spent years trying to find the
perfect chocolate chip recipe. I combined elements from my favorites to create an LBL original that is always a crowd pleaser,
especially with Team FEED (FEED Projects is the philanthropic
business I founded in 2007). I suggest using all-natural ingredients to make this delicious snack—I mean dessert—a more
palatable option for a health-conscious group.

Chocolate Chip Cookies

Makes about 4½ dozen

6 ounces (1½ sticks) unsalted
  butter, melted and cooled slightly,
  more for the cookie sheets

1 cup organic brown sugar

½ cup organic raw cane sugar

1 large egg

1 large egg yolk

1 tablespoon vanilla extract

2½ cups organic all-purpose flour

1 teaspoon baking soda

½ teaspoon fine sea salt

10 ounces dark chocolate chips
  (1⅔ cups)

1. Preheat the oven to 375°F and butter 2 large cookie sheets.

2. In a large bowl, stir together the melted butter, brown sugar, and raw
cane sugar. Stir in the egg, egg yolk, and vanilla.

3. In a separate bowl, whisk together the flour, baking soda, and salt.
Stir into the batter. Fold in the chocolate chips.

4. Put tablespoon-sized balls of dough on the cookie sheets, about 1 inch
apart and press flat.

5. Bake 1 sheet at a time until cookies are pale golden, about 7 minutes.
(Take out before they turn golden brown; cookies will continue to cook
on cookie sheet.) Put the sheet on a rack to cool, then remove cookies
directly to the rack to cool completely.

CHUCK PIEKARSKI

Pastry chef

To be truthful, I had no idea what God's Love We Deliver was when I answered their employment ad in a local New York City paper. During my first interview, I was told of the important contribution the organization was making to the HIV/AIDS community. Having lost my dear companion to the virus only four years earlier, I knew immediately it would be a wonderful and fulfilling place to work. In the spring of 1991 I happily started baking for God's Love—almost 300 desserts a day!

Here is a story that I think exemplifies the impact of the efforts we make here at God's Love. Back when the AIDS crisis was at its peak, I was manning an outreach booth for GLWD at a local street fair. As I handed out fliers and told people of the services we offered, a woman approached me and shared the fact that she was once a recipient of our meal delivery program. She told me how GLWD saved her life by providing her with wonderful meals that she could never have otherwise afforded, and went on to say that our desserts in particular had helped her through some very dark days,

reminding her of the sweets her mother had made with love. Then she said: "If you see the baker, please thank him for me." I told her who I was, and after a moment of silence she gave me the longest, most sincere, tear-filled hug of my life. She then very enthusiastically began to list her favorite GLWD desserts: chocolate oatmeal cookies, applesauce cake, cinnamon-raisin scones, fudge brownies ... As we talked she let me know how much better she was feeling and how she was planning to start volunteering soon at a nearby food pantry. She wanted to give back—to those who might be struggling and in need of a hand, as she once had been. Our meeting was humbling, yet it also made me quietly proud to think of all the lives I'd had the opportunity to touch through God's Love.

Today, God's Love We Deliver reaches a much wider range of clients with varied needs. I am now creating more than 2500 desserts per day. Fifteen million meals and 25 years later, I am honored to say I'm still the pastry chef at GLWD—but I prefer the title "Chuck the Baker."

Double-Chocolate Oatmeal Cookies

Makes about 4 dozen cookies

1¼ cups all-purpose flour

4½ tablespoons cocoa powder

1 teaspoon baking soda

4 ounces (1 stick) butter or
  margarine, softened

¾ cup light brown sugar

½ cup granulated sugar

2 large eggs

1 teaspoon vanilla extract

3 cups rolled oats

1 cup chocolate chips

1. Preheat the oven to 350°F.

2. In a bowl, whisk together the flour, cocoa powder, and baking soda to blend.

3. Using an electric mixer, beat the butter and sugars until blended. Add the eggs and vanilla and beat until incorporated. Add the flour mixture and beat until just incorporated. Fold in the oats and chocolate chips.

4. Drop rounded tablespoons of dough onto parchment- or silicon-lined cookie sheets about 1 inch apart and bake, 1 sheet at a time, until golden brown, 8 to 10 minutes per batch. Transfer the cookies to racks to cool.

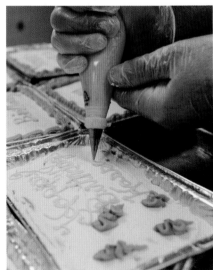

AFTERWORD

The stories in this cookbook illustrate what we know to be true—so much love is given and received through the simple act of preparing a meal, a dish, or a dessert for someone who touches your heart. We experience this every day at God's Love We Deliver. We believe that Food is Love; it's a way to take care of our clients when they need us most.

Food is Medicine for our clients as well. Our meals help them heal, feel stronger, and stay as healthy as they can for as long as possible. For so many, it's the difference between staying in their home, where they want to be, instead of going to a hospital or long-term care facility.

Together, Food is Love and Food is Medicine make up the most powerful recipe there is for those living with a life-altering illness. And that's what this cookbook makes possible.

I am exceedingly proud of this project. With the support of so many contributors and underwriters, what started as a "good idea" has become a powerful tool for sharing the passion of many important friends of God's Love. Together, the contributors have shared their stories and family recipes, helping to raise visibility and resources for the life-sustaining mission of God's Love.

I thank everyone who has made this cookbook a reality. I offer special thanks to Jon Gilman, our dedicated board member, and Christopher Idone, a longtime volunteer, for conceiving the project and getting it started. Jon almost single-handedly moved this beautiful book from idea to fruition; his commitment to God's Love is heroic, and we are grateful for his efforts.

In August 2015, God's Love We Deliver moved into the new Michael Kors Building, allowing us to more than double the number of meals we cook and home deliver each year. We are excited by our expanded capacity to reach so many more people in great need, and to bring them the nutritionally tailored and delicious meals that help them manage their illness and improve their quality of life.

I hope you'll join us in reaching those who count on God's Love for their meals, by volunteering and/or donating. You will be joining a wonderful community of people who, every day, deliver hope, dignity, respect, and love to thousands of people when they are so sick that they cannot shop or cook for themselves.

KAREN PEARL, President & CEO, God's Love We Deliver

TIMELINE

1985

Hospice volunteer Ganga Stone delivers groceries to Richard, a man living with AIDS. He is too ill to prepare the packaged food she has brought him. She realizes that a meal, not groceries, is what people need when they are sick.

1986

God's Love We Deliver is co-founded by Ganga Stone and Jane Best. Restaurant Claire begins donating prepared meals that Ganga and volunteers deliver—many by bicycle—to people living with AIDS in Manhattan. Other restaurants join in. Ganga and volunteers deliver an average of 50 meals per week.

1990

Bloomingdales offers to cook the Thanksgiving turkeys for clients due to the lack of kitchen space at God's Love We Deliver, and Bid of Love Art Auction at Sotheby's raises $600,000 for God's Love We Deliver.

1991

The demand for services continues to grow. By this time, God's Love is serving 250 clients per day. Chuck "The Baker" Piekarski joins the staff and creates the recipe for Chuck's Famous Brownies. Chuck starts baking and decorating a personalized birthday cake for every client with their name piped in frosting. Mayor Dinkins initiates the mayoral tradition of delivering Thanksgiving meals. God's Love We Deliver receives first funding from the Ryan White CARE Act and moves to a larger rented kitchen space at the American Youth Hostel at Amsterdam Avenue and 103rd Street.

1992

God's Love We Deliver establishes its Nutrition Department to help people living with HIV/AIDS and their caregivers receive information about the importance of nutrition to compromised immune systems. God's Love starts delivering two meals a day (lunch and dinner) with the help of its first delivery van, donated by the Manhattan Borough President's office. Friends Seminary in Manhattan begins the tradition of schoolchildren hand-decorating shopping bags in which God's Love We Deliver holiday meals are delivered.

1993

As growth continues and God's Love finds itself out of space, it successfully bids on a vacant building located at the corner of Spring Street and Avenue of the Americas. David Geffen provides a gift of $1.5 million to renovate the building. The Nutrition Department publishes the first of its many important eating and nutrition guides: *Living with HIV: A Nutrition Guide with Special Emphasis for People in Recovery.*

1994

God's Love We Deliver initiates yearly fundraising events with the First Annual Race to Deliver.

1995

God's Love delivers its 1 millionth meal. God's Love We Deliver moves into its new home in SoHo on World AIDS DAY, December 1.

1996

Ceramic wall tiles are sold as a fundraiser and are installed in the new SoHo kitchen.

1997

God's Love delivers its 2 millionth meal.

2000

R&B singer Mary J. Blige presents a check to God's Love We Deliver for $50,000 on behalf of the MAC AIDS Fund. God's Love now delivers, on average, to more than 1,000 clients per day. God's Love We Deliver launches the first annual Midsummer Night Drinks. The party is hosted by Alan Rogers in Southampton.

2001

God's Love We Deliver expands its mission to serve clients living with serious illnesses other than HIV/AIDS. God's Love delivers its 5 millionth meal and begins delivery of frozen meals. God's Love prepares and delivers more than 3,000 meals for search-and-rescue workers in the days following September 11. The Swatch "Wristory" auction raises $720,000 to help cover post-9/11 fundraising gaps.

2004

God's Love We Deliver moves its kitchen to Long Island City while it renovates its SoHo kitchen. The renovation improves capacity by 66 percent and lays the infrastructure for future growth. God's Love We Deliver reaches the milestone of more than 1,200 active volunteers each month.

2005

God's Love We Deliver initiates a program for breast cancer clients and pilots the caregiver meals program.

2006

God's Love We Deliver celebrates its 20th Anniversary.

2007

In the wake of a Valentine's Day snowstorm, God's Love We Deliver raises more than $34,000 in one afternoon to fund two emergency Blizzard Boxes filled with nonperishable food for each client.

2008

At the 2nd Annual Golden Heart Awards dinner, God's Love We Deliver honors Harry Slatkin, 7th On Sale, and longtime volunteer Roz Gilbert. God's Love We Deliver cooks and delivers more than 800,000 meals this year to 3,635 clients, a 20-percent increase from the previous year.

2009

God's Love We Deliver commemorates the delivery of its 10 millionth meal with an event that includes agency founder Ganga Stone, CEO Karen Pearl, Blaine Trump, Joan Rivers, Estée Lauder Group President John Demsey, Anna Wintour, and many other notable guests. Further, to meet the changing needs of its clients, God's Love moves forward with a plan to deliver more chilled and frozen meals. This is made possible by generous grants from Feeding America and the Judith C. White Foundation.

2010

God's Love is a winner of the prestigious New York Times Company Nonprofit Excellence Award and rolls out an enhanced children's menu. Breakfasts include cold cereals, oatmeal, low-fat milk, yogurt, raisins, and fruits, while dinner has "child-sized" portions of "kid-friendly" food such as turkey meatballs and spaghetti, along with fruit and desserts. A daily snack of soup, a granola bar, fruit, cheese, and other healthy items is designed to help children keep their nourishment up after school.

2011

God's Love kicks off its 25-year anniversary by ringing the NASDAQ Closing Bell on April 7. God's Love reaches an agency record and delivers more than 1 million meals in one year for the first time ever, for a grand total of 1,000,732 meals. As the demand for services continues to reach record numbers each year, the need for an expanded building becomes urgent. In response, God's Love We Deliver launches a multi-million-dollar expansion campaign.

2012

At the Sixth Annual Golden Heart Awards, Michael Kors, the world-renowned award-winning designer, announces a $5-million gift to the Expansion Campaign. In honor of this donation, the new building will be named the Michael Kors Building at God's Love We Deliver. With additional significant contributions from New York City, Steven and Alex Cohen, Jeff Gates and Mike Moran, and Chris Lacovara and Sam Green, the funding campaign for the new building is in high gear. In the wake of Hurricane Sandy's destruction, God's Love delivers 8,000 meals to people displaced by Sandy and 2,300 emergency meal kits called "Sandy Bags" to its clients.

2013

God's Love moves to a temporary home in Brooklyn as work begins on the new headquarters in SoHo.

2014

God's Love We Deliver commemorates the delivery of its 15 millionth meal with an event that includes Brooklyn Borough President Eric Adams; New York City Council members Corey Johnson and Robert Cornegy; Sylvia Vogelman, a 22-year volunteer with more than 2,800 hours of service; board member Linda Fairstein; Michael Sennott, former board chair and current chair of the Expansion Campaign; and the incomparable Joan Rivers. God's Love announces that, in honor of Joan and her 20-plus years of dedicated service and her love of Chuck's sweet treats, the bakery in the new building will be named the Joan Rivers Bakery.

2015

On June 9, 2015, Michael Kors, Anna Wintour, and Melissa Rivers join Mayor Bill de Blasio and other notable New Yorkers as well as God's Love staff, donors, and volunteers to celebrate the dedication of the Michael Kors Building. The brand-new state-of-the-art 9,600 square-foot kitchen on the second floor has wonderful natural light and includes four industrial-size refrigerators, three freezers, five blast freezers, five 80-gallon soup kettles, and a waste digester that converts up to 1,000 pounds of organic food waste into disposable water. Every day, more and more sick and hungry New Yorkers reach out to God's Love, looking for help. The new building allows God's Love to continue to respond to the urgent needs of its clients for years to come.

Chuck's Brownies

Makes 588 (3 x 3-inch) brownies

If you ever find yourself at the corner of Spring Street and 6th Avenue in Manhattan's SoHo, and the sweet smell of chocolate is in the air, that probably means Chuck the Baker is making his brownies again. Each year, with the help of his favorite Hobart mixer and hundreds of volunteers, Chuck bakes up more than 20,000 brownies. They have become a signature gift from God's Love We Deliver, available year-round. The recipe that follows gives a sense of what goes in to preparing just one batch, about 600 brownies.

50 pounds semisweet
   chocolate chips

16 pounds unsalted butter

10 cups hot water

64 cups granulated sugar

14–16 dozen eggs,
   depending on size

1½ cups vanilla extract

8 tablespoons baking powder

6 tablespoons baking soda

6 tablespoons salt

64 cups all-purpose flour

1. Preheat oven to 325°F.

2. In a large pot over low heat, melt 45 pounds of the chocolate chips and butter together, stirring occasionally.

3. Pour the melted chocolate and butter into the mixing bowl of a large standing mixer. Add the hot water and mix just until smooth. Add the sugar and mix just until smooth. Add the eggs and vanilla and mix just until smooth. Combine all the dry ingredients, add to the batter and mix just until incorporated. Fold in the remaining 5 pounds of chocolate chips.

4. Pour the batter into 21 hotel-sized baking pans (approximately 20 by12 by 2 inches) and bake for 40 to 50 minutes in a convection oven. Gently turn the pans about halfway through the bake time. The middle will rise while baking; when the middle sinks down again, the brownies are done. If you like cakier brownies, bake another 4 to 5 minutes. Remove from oven and allow brownies to cool in pan.

5. Cut into approximately 3-inch squares and serve.

INDEX

CREDITS

ACKNOWLEDGMENTS

There are so many people to thank who helped to lift and support this project.

At its inception, of course there was my dear friend Christopher Idone, the acclaimed cookbook author, who loved the idea from the very beginning and, through his expertise, gave me the confidence to take on the challenge.

Joe Dolce, a talented writer and one of my oldest friends, helped me to organize my thoughts into an initial presentation and has been a terrific sounding board and champion throughout.

Early on, I called upon our wonderful Sag Harbor neighbor, Esther Newberg, the legendary literary agent, who, over a Sunday-morning coffee, listened to my first pitch. She loved the idea and challenged me to get five people from our wish list to commit, at which time she would lead us through the process. She has remained steadfast ever since and has also brought in some incredible contributors.

I can't thank those first five enough, who all said yes without hesitation—Isabella Rossellini, Ina Garten, Danny Meyer, Katie Workman, and Michael Kors.

And so, the adventure began…

Christopher called his dear friend Lena Tabori of Welcome Enterprises, Inc., who graciously offered to advise us and package the book. Her guidance has been invaluable.

Ben Fink, the celebrated food photographer and videographer, offered us his time, support, and talent over nearly two years, all for his love of the organization. He conceived and created the beautiful images that illustrate each recipe, and directed the accompanying videos for the book.

The creation of this book is truly an example of how sometimes too many cooks in the kitchen make for a great feast. My heartfelt gratitude goes out to:

Michael Anthony, fellow board member and Executive Chef at Gramercy Tavern and Untitled at the Whitney, and his assistant Beth Wisniewski, who helped connect us to so many of the stellar group of chefs included in the book.

Shelley Wiseman, our recipe tester, who was instrumental in planning, organizing, and executing every dish that was photographed.

Joe Tully, for his artistic eye and for lending a hand in styling.

Friend, neighbor, and great cook Lesley Sondey, for her generosity and tireless energy in the kitchen during all the shoots.

Laura Thorne, Linda Vacey, and Alan Gottlich at Party Rental Ltd., for all their help and encouragement and the generous use of so many great props.

Laura and John Smith of Serene Green in Sag Harbor, and the many farmers and purveyors on Eastern Long Island for their amazing produce and dedication to the slow-food movement.

Katrina Fried, our incredible editor, who has spent hours each week on the phone with me guiding this project with such ease, skill, and finesse.

Gregory Wakabayashi, our art director, whose expertise and keen eye brought the pages to life.

LaMont Craig, who has assisted me for the last two and a half years, week after week, always with a smile on his face; his perseverance and many great ideas were highly motivating, especially during those weeks when it seemed like we would never get to the finish line.

My husband, Brad Learmonth, for all the hours of help and for listening to me doubt, bitch, and gush—this truly was a product of love.

The board and staff of God's Love We Deliver, but especially Chief Development Officer David Ludwigson and our CEO Karen Pearl, who embraced the idea of the book and have supported it all the way.

The 76 contributors who stepped up on the first ask and gave us stories and recipes from their hearts.

Many, many thanks to all those who helped bring in contributors and to all the friends who lent their support in countless ways, particularly: Janette Beckman, Mark Brashear, Joanne Cassullo, Beth Rudin Dewoody, David Drumgold, John Esty, Richard Feldman, Pat Fili, Henny Garfunkel, April Gornik, Lori Griffith, Deirdre Guest, Mark and Blythe Harris, Anne Keating, Michael Kors, Gregory Lewis, Lock McKelvy, Laura Michalchyshyn, Georgia Oetker, Steven and Stephanie Reiner, Liz Reid, Alicia Rodriguez, Mary Salter, Zoe Sandler, Dawn Sheggeby, Sal Siggia, Ward Simmons, Alice Turner, Billy Weiner, Ken Wright, and the many others who have encouraged, listened, and offered assistance and suggestions.

Last, but certainly never least, this book is a tribute to all the volunteers, staff, supporters, and, especially, clients who inspire us to do this important work each and every day. Thank you for your tireless commitment and compassion.

I toast you all,

JON GILMAN

GOD'S LOVE WE DELIVER COOKBOOK
Nourishing Stories and Recipes from Notable Friends
Compiled by Jon Gilman and Christopher Idone
Introduction by Ina Garten
Food Photography by Ben Fink

Published in 2016 by God's Love We Deliver
166 Avenue of the Americas, New York, N.Y. 10013
(212) 294-8100
www.glwd.org
For bulk and special sales requests, please contact cookbook@glwd.org
or write us (c/o godslovewedelivercookbook) at the above address.

Produced by Welcome Enterprises, Inc.
6 West 18th Street, 4B, New York, N.Y. 10011
(212) 989-3200; Fax (212) 989-3205
www.welcomeenterprisesinc.com

Project Director: Lena Tabori
Editor: Katrina Fried
Designer: Gregory Wakabayashi

Addtional copyright and credit information on page 293

Every reasaonable effort has been made to trace the copyright holders of the
photographs in this book but one or two were unreachable. We would be grateful
if the photographers concerned would contact us.

If you notice an error, please alert us by emailing cookbook@glwd.org.
We will post corrections on the website listed below.

Library of Congress Cataloging-in-Publication Data on file

ISBN 978-0-9652128-0-9
First Edition

10 9 8 7 6 5 4 3 2 1
Printed in China by Toppan Leefung

For further information about this book please visit online:
www.glwd.org/cookbook